Reading Comprehension

Grade 4

ISBN 978-0-544-26768-8

1 2 3 4 5 6 7 8 9 10 XXXX 22 21 20 19 18 17 16 15 14 13

4500000000 B C D E F G

Dear Parent,

Welcome to the *Core Skills Reading Comprehension* series! You have selected a unique book that focuses on developing your child's comprehension skills, the reading and thinking processes associated with the printed word. Because this series was designed by experienced reading professionals, your child will have reading success as well as gain a firm understanding of the necessary skills outlined in national standards.

Reading should be a fun, relaxed activity for children. They should read selections that relate to or build on their own experiences. Vocabulary should be presented in a sequential and logical progression. The selections in this series build on these philosophies to insure your child's reading success. Other important features in this series that will further aid your child include:

- Short reading selections of interest to a young reader.

- Vocabulary introduced in context and repeated often.

- Comprehension skills applied in context to make the reading more relevant.

- Multiple-choice exercises that develop skills for standardized test taking.

You may wish to have your child read the selections silently or orally, but you will find that sharing the selections and activities with your child will provide additional confidence and support to succeed. When learners experience success, learning becomes a continuous process moving them onward to higher achievements. Moreover, the more your child reads, the more proficient she or he will become.

Enjoy this special time with your child!

Sincerely,
The Educators and Staff of Houghton Mifflin Harcourt

Core Skills Reading Comprehension
GRADE 4

Table of Contents

Table of Contents

Core Skills Reading Comprehension, Grade 4

Skills Correlation

LANGUAGE ARTS SKILLS	SELECTION
LITERATURE SKILLS	
Cause and Effect	1, 2
Character, Setting, Plot	1, 2, 6
Compare and Contrast Literary Works	2, Skills Review: Selections 1–6
Details and Inferences	1, 2, 5, 7, 11, 12
Drawing Conclusions	1, 5
Facts and Opinions	12, Skills Review: Selections 7–12
Graphic Sources	6, Skills Review: Selections 1–6
Main Idea and Supporting Details	6, Skills Review: Selections 1–6, 12
Make Connections	2, Skills Review: Selections 1–6
Narrator	5
Predicting Outcomes	6, 7
Sequencing	5, 11
Text Structure	7
Theme	1
INFORMATIONAL TEXT SKILLS	
Cause and Effect	10
Compare and Contrast Accounts of Events	4
Details and Inferences	3, 8, 9, 10, Skills Review: Selections 7–12
Explain Events, Procedures, Ideas or Concepts	9, 10, Skills Review: Selections 7–12
Integrate Information	4, 10
Main Idea and Supporting Details	4, 8, Skills Review: Selections 1–6
Reason and Evidence	10
Sequencing	9, Skills Review: Selections 7–12
Summary	8
Text Structure	9, 10
Visuals in Informational Texts	9, 10

© Houghton Mifflin Harcourt Publishing Company

Skills Correlation, continued

LANGUAGE ARTS SKILLS	SELECTION
VOCABULARY AND DECODING	
Classifying	2
Dictionary	7, 10, Skills Review: Selections 7–12
Idioms	6, Skills Review: Selections 1–6, 12
Multiple-Meaning Words	7, Skills Review: Selections 7–12
Picture Clues	3
Synonyms	3, Skills Review: Selections 7–12
Word Meaning	5, 6, 8, 9, 11, 12
Words in Context	1, 2, 7, 9
RESEARCH AND STUDY SKILLS	
Encyclopedia	10
Outlining	8

Selection 1: Paired

Why the Crocodile Has a Bumpy Back
a folktale from Angola

Long ago the crocodile's back was as soft and smooth as a little child's cheek. One evening the crocodile was relaxing beside the river. Suddenly the rabbit came sprinting along and bumped right into him.

"Rabbit," said the crocodile, "why do you wake me? And why are you all out of breath?"

"I have been running all morning from the dog," the rabbit panted. "A man sent him to chase me. I think the man wants to have *me* for his dinner!" Suddenly the rabbit had a thought that made him nervous. "You're not hungry, are you?" he asked the crocodile.

"No," said the weary crocodile, his eyelids barely opening. "I've already eaten my dinner."

"That's good," said the rabbit with a sigh of relief. "I've had enough trouble for one day."

"Well," said the crocodile, "I never have trouble. In fact, I bet Trouble would be afraid to bother me."

"I don't think you should talk like that," the rabbit warned him. "Trouble might not like you to talk about it that way."

The rabbit bounded off, but the crocodile could not stop thinking about what he had said. The more he reflected on the rabbit's words, the more angry he became. Finally, he decided to go find Trouble and tell him to mind his own business.

The crocodile frightened the flamingo, who was wading in the river. She flew up in the air and startled the monkey, who had just lit the candles on his friend's birthday cake. The monkey jumped away to hide, knocking over the cake and setting fire to the tall, dry grass.

As the flames grew higher and higher around him, the crocodile ran to throw himself into the river. By the time he reached the safety of the cool water, his back was burned and rough.

Ever since then, the crocodile's back has been bumpy, and he's been a grumpy fellow.

Ⓐ Circle the correct answer for each question.

1. Why did the rabbit ask the crocodile if he was hungry?
   a. Rabbit did not like to watch the crocodile eat.
   b. Rabbit knew it was not polite to interrupt dinner.
   c. Rabbit was afraid the crocodile would eat him.
   d. Rabbit didn't want the dog to catch him.

2. What is a summary of the plot of this selection?
   a. Crocodile avoids trouble and gets burned.
   b. Crocodile looks for Trouble, causes trouble, and burns his back.
   c. Crocodile looks for Trouble and gets a big reward.
   d. Crocodile follows the rabbit, avoids trouble, and burns his back.

3. What causes the fire in the selection?

    a. The monkey knocks over the cake with burning candles.

    b. The crocodile startles the monkey by running to the river.

    c. The flamingo flies to the tree and knocks over the candles.

    d. The man with the dog chases the rabbit up the tree.

4. Read the following sentences from the selection.

> "Well," said the crocodile, "I never have trouble. In fact, I bet Trouble would be afraid to bother me."

Why does the author use a capital *T* in the word *Trouble*?

    a. because Crocodile thinks "Trouble" is someone's name

    b. because "Trouble" is the name of the flamingo

    c. because "Trouble" is the name of the monkey

    d. because Crocodile thinks "Trouble" is the name of the river

5. What word in the selection helps the reader understand the meaning of *sprinting*?

    a. *taking*

    b. *running*

    c. *thinking*

    d. *knocking*

6. How was the rabbit talking when he panted, "I have been running all morning from the dog"?

    a. too fast to be understood

    b. with laughter as he said each word

    c. in a hoarse voice as if he had a cold

    d. as if he were out of breath

3

Name _____ Date _____

B **Read each sentence. Find two words in the box that can be substituted for the underlined word or words. Write them on the line under the sentence.**

afraid	considered	nervous	sleepy
bounded	grouchy	reflected	splashing
bumpy	grumpy	relaxing	wading
calming	hopped	rough	weary

1. Usually, a small animal will feel <u>fearful</u> at the sight of a crocodile.

   _____

2. When the rabbit heard the barking of the dog, it <u>leapt</u> away in a hurry.

   _____

3. The <u>tired</u> crocodile yawned and stretched out in the shade for an afternoon nap.

   _____

4. Flamingos spend much of their day <u>walking in shallow water</u>.

   _____

5. As the crocodile <u>thought</u> about it, he believed Trouble was a person or animal.

   _____

6. "There is nothing more <u>restful</u> than lying beside a river and listening to the rhythm of the water," said the crocodile.

   _____

7. When the boat approached, the crocodile bared his teeth to show how <u>unpleasant</u> he felt.

   _____

8. Both crocodiles and alligators have <u>uneven</u> skin on their backs.

   _____

4

Selection 1: Paired
Core Skills Reading Comprehension, Grade 4

C Why something happens is a *cause*. What happens is an *effect*. Complete the chart about events in "Why the Crocodile Has a Bumpy Back" by adding causes and effects.

Cause	Effect
1.	The crocodile grows angry.
The crocodile frightens the wading flamingo.	2.
The monkey jumps away from the flamingo.	3.
4.	The crocodile throws himself into the river.
5.	The crocodile's back is now bumpy.

5

Name _____ Date _____

D An author describes a character's appearance, words, and actions. Find text evidence to support the ideas about the crocodile. Use the evidence to complete the chart.

Crocodile	Text Examples or Quotations	What the Example or Quotation Tells About the Character
Appearance	1. _____ _____ _____ _____ 2. _____ _____ _____ _____	The crocodile's appearance changes in the selection.
Words	3. _____ _____ _____ _____	When the crocodile is upset, he says how he feels.
Actions	4. _____ _____ _____ _____	The crocodile is confused about a word's meaning.

E **Every selection has at least one theme. The theme of a selection is the big idea. Usually, an author does not state the theme. The reader must figure it out.**

Think about the theme of "Why the Crocodile Has a Bumpy Back." The theme is shown on the web below. Find three ideas in the selection that support the theme.

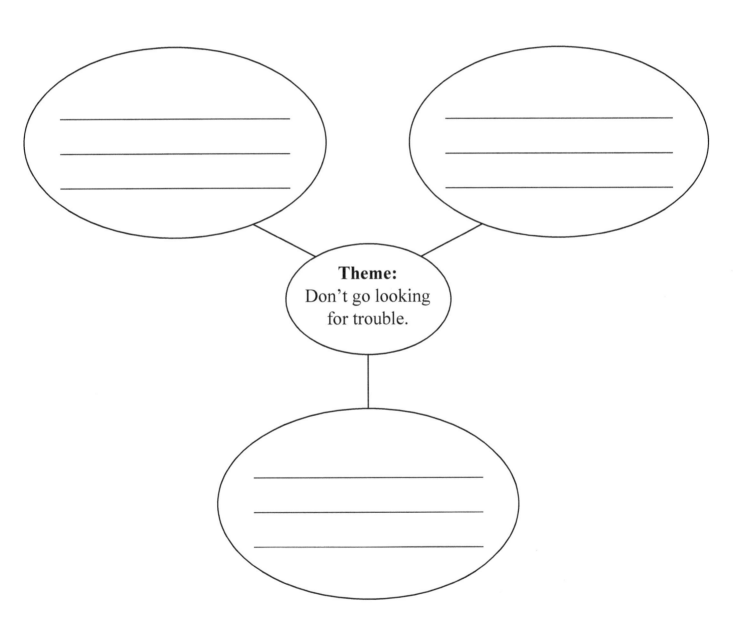

Theme:
Don't go looking
for trouble.

Selection 2: Paired

How the Chipmunk Got Its Stripes

One evening, a very long time ago, a bear was out walking. This was back when animals could speak and before chipmunks had stripes down their backs.

"I can do anything, anything, anything," chanted Bear as he walked. "I can do anything, anything at all!"

"Really?" asked a little chipmunk.

"Why, yes," said Bear. "I am the strongest animal. I can do anything I want to do."

"Can you stop the sun from rising in the morning?" asked Chipmunk.

"Of course I can," Bear answered.

"Are you sure?" asked Chipmunk with a sly smile.

"I am very sure," said Bear.

It grew dark and stars began to appear in the night sky. Bear sat down facing east where the sun had risen that morning and every other morning as far back as he could remember.

Chipmunk snuggled down into his hole in the ground, laughing himself to sleep at how foolish Bear was.

But Bear did not sleep. He told the sun, "Do not come up in the morning." He said it over and over again all night.

Finally, after many hours, Chipmunk climbed out of his hole in the ground and sat next to Bear. "The sun will rise," whispered Chipmunk.

"The sun will not rise!" exclaimed Bear, but there was already a golden glow in the east. "Do not rise!" He ordered the sun, but the sun did not obey.

8

"Look!" Chipmunk shouted. "It's the sunrise!"

Bear was very upset. This was the first time in his life he had not gotten his way.

Chipmunk was happy. He jumped up and down, singing, "The sun came up. The sun came up."

This made Bear even more angry. Quick as lightning, Bear shot out one big paw and pinned Chipmunk to the ground. "Perhaps I cannot stop the sun," he said, "but I can stop you."

Chipmunk realized that he was in big trouble now. "Oh, Bear," he said. "I was just kidding. Please let me go."

But Bear did not move his paw. His claws pressed into Chipmunk's back.

"Look!" Chipmunk yelled. "The sun changed its mind. It is going back down."

Bear turned to see if he had won after all, but the sun was exactly where it always was at the time of morning.

Chipmunk had tricked Bear into looking away. Bear's paw moved a little too. It was just enough for Chipmunk to squirm free. But the tips of Bear's claws scraped painfully all the way down Chipmunk's back.

Chipmunk ran as fast as he could back to the safety of his hole in the ground. Eventually, Chipmunk's back healed, but there were three long scars where Bear's claws had scratched him. This is how Chipmunk got his stripes.

Now, all chipmunks have stripes down their backs. Maybe the stripes are there as a reminder of what can happen when one animal teases another.

9

A **Circle the correct answer for each question.**

1. What character trait was Bear showing as he chanted "I can do anything, anything at all!"?

   a. thoughtful

   b. sad

   c. boastful

   d. likeable

2. Why does Chipmunk have a sly smile when he says, "Are you sure?" to Bear?

   a. He means the opposite of what he is saying.

   b. He knows Bear can't control the sun.

   c. He sees the sun coming up in the distance.

   d. He does not understand what Bear is saying.

3. Why did Bear stay awake all night?

   a. Bear was keeping his eye on Chipmunk.

   b. Bear was talking to the moon.

   c. Bear was trying to scratch Chipmunk.

   d. Bear was chanting to the sun.

4. What happened right after Chipmunk woke up?

   a. The bear bragged.

   b. The sun rose in the sky.

   c. The sky grew dark.

   d. Chipmunk laughed at Bear.

5. Look at the picture of the chipmunk on page 9. What text from the selection best describes the picture?

   a. *This was back when animals could speak and before chipmunks had stripes down their backs.*

   b. *Chipmunk snuggled down into his hole in the ground, laughing himself to sleep at how foolish Bear was.*

   c. *Chipmunk realized that he was in big trouble now.*

   d. *Eventually, Chipmunk's back healed, but there were three long scars where Bear's claws had scratched him. This is how Chipmunk got his stripes.*

Name _____ Date _____

B This selection tells why chipmunks have stripes. Why something happens is a *cause*. What happens is an *effect*. Complete the chart by adding causes and effects.

Cause	Effect
1.	Chipmunk laughs himself to sleep.
2.	Bear is very upset.
By saying "The sun came up," Chipmunk makes Bear angry.	3.
Chipmunk tricks Bear into looking at the sun.	4.
5.	Chipmunk has three scars on his back.

11

C **Find the word that best matches the definition. Write the word on the line.**

glow	rise
healed	snuggled
reminder	squirm

_____ 1. when a wound or injury becomes healthy again

_____ 2. to twist from side to side to get away from being held

_____ 3. moved into a warm, comfortable position

_____ 4. a low, steady light

_____ 5. something that helps one remember something

_____ 6. go upwards

Now choose a word from the box to complete each sentence. Write the word on the line.

7. Each table in the restaurant had a _____ from the lit candles.

8. Have you ever tried to hold a puppy that is trying to _____ out of your arms?

9. My broken leg _____ slowly wrapped in a cast.

10. Jorge wrote a _____ on his calendar about Friday's test.

11. Mia _____ into her sleeping bag on the camping trip.

12. I let go of the balloon and watched it

_____ over the rooftops.

12

Name _____ Date _____

D Complete each web with words and phrases to describe each character.

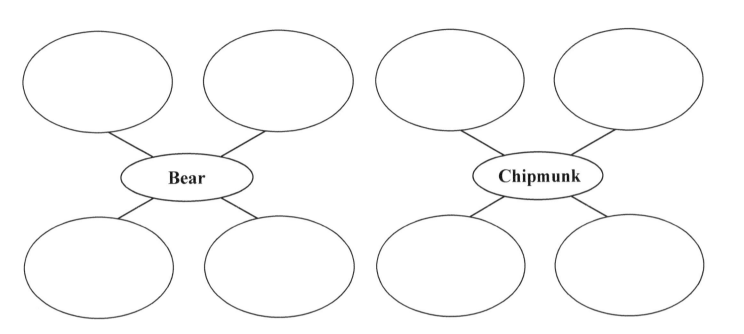

Use the information from each web to write a description of each character.

Bear

_____

_____

_____

_____

Chipmunk

_____

_____

_____

_____

13

E **List three items for each category.**

1. Animals That Live Underground

_____

_____

_____

2. Things with Stripes

_____

_____

_____

3. Animals with Claws

_____

_____

_____

4. Objects in the Sky

_____

_____

_____

14

F **Circle the correct answer for each question.**

1. What familiar theme, or big idea, is found in selections 1 and 2?

   a. Honesty is the best policy.

   b. To have a friend, you must be a friend.

   c. Sometimes you must learn a lesson the hard way.

   d. Beauty is only skin-deep.

2. What similar emotion did the crocodile in selection 1 and Bear in selection 2 feel?

   a. fear

   b. anger

   c. loneliness

   d. surprise

3. What do the titles of selections 1 and 2 tell you about the folktales?

   a. Both stories will explain how something in nature came to be.

   b. Both stories have good and bad characters.

   c. Both stories have characters with magical powers.

   d. Both stories take place in the same setting.

4. In what way are the main characters in selections 1 and 2 alike?

   a. They both are scary, dangerous animals.

   b. They both have homes underground.

   c. They both make new friends.

   d. They both change the way they look.

5. What kind of texts are selections 1 and 2?

   a. biographies   c. plays

   b. folktales   d. science fiction

6. When do "Why the Crocodile Has a Bumpy Back" and "How the Chipmunk Got Its Stripes" take place?

   a. present day

   b. midday

   c. long ago

   d. in the future

15

G The plot, or story events, in selections 1 and 2 follows a problem-and-solution pattern. Complete the story map to identify each story's problem, how the character tries to solve the problem, the character's solution, and the story ending.

	"Why the Crocodile Has a Bumpy Back"	"How the Chipmunk Got Its Stripes"
Character	Crocodile	Chipmunk
Problem	1. _____ _____	4. _____ _____
Events	2. _____ _____ _____ _____ _____	5. _____ _____ _____ _____ _____
Solution	Crocodile jumps into the river.	Bear looks away and Chipmunk squirms free.
Story Ending	3. _____ _____	6. _____ _____

Selection 3: Paired

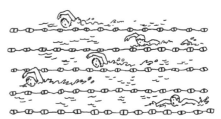

June 18

Dear Grandma,

    I felt like a wilted flower at the pool today. Even my friend Rudy Gómez noticed and asked what was wrong. I lost the swim race again! That's my fourth loss of the summer!

    Rudy wants me to be like him and not enter the swim races and just swim for exercise. Rudy's mother was a champion tennis player so he never played tennis. But, swimming runs in our family! With Mom as a swimming coach and Dad as the star of his college swim team, I want to swim like Hannah. Hannah has a shelf full of diving trophies and medals and is thinking about the Olympics. I want to be able to compete like my sister!

    Do you have any advice for me, Grandma?

Love,
Wayne

June 22

Dear Wayne,

    Practice makes perfect! Try harder. Work at it longer. I know you can do it.

Love,
Grandma

July 3

Dear Grandma,

    I am following your advice. I practice every day. Every morning, I swim laps over and over again. My diving is still clumsy and my speed is not improving.

    I think Claire is half-girl, half-fish. Here she is, just four years old and she went from the Tadpole class to the Minnow class. Her teacher said, "I've never seen a child learn so quickly." I think she'll be moving to the Codfish class and swimming in deep water soon. Now, I am proud of my little sister but she's going to pass me by.

With love from the swimming moose,
Wayne

July 10

Dear Wayne,

You are a strong swimmer, but maybe you should stop entering swimming races. Everyone has different talents, and I don't want you to be jealous of your sisters' ability to swim.

Think about other things you are good at.

Love,
Grandma

August 15

Dear Grandma,

I came in third place in last week's swim meet! I am still practicing every day. Unfortunately, I came in last in this week's race.

Did you hear that Hannah won two more first place medals? And, Claire has moved up to Dolphin. She's a natural in the pool!

School starts soon, but I am still going to keep swimming. I just have to win once! Just one time.

Love,
Wayne

September 10

Dear Wayne,

I am proud of you. You don't give up easily. I think you should keep swimming for the enjoyment and exercise. It sounds like time to stop entering swimming races.

Love,
Grandma

October 29

Dear Grandma,

Today was quite a day! Sailing ships from other countries were anchored in the harbor, and Mr. Clemente took the class on a field trip to see them. I was excited to see them since I love sailing on your little boat when we visit you.

After we toured the ship from Norway, we were lined up on the dock while Mr. Clemente made sure we were in pairs. (I was paired with my buddy Rudy Gómez, of course.) I noticed a houseboat that was docking. A baby girl toddled on the deck. I looked for an adult but no one was near.

I yelled, "Somebody get the baby!" But no one heard me over the crowd noise and boat motors. Then, she fell into the deep water!

I didn't even think. I just kicked off my shoes, made one of my clumsy dives, and went in after her. My practice paid off—I may not be fast, but I am strong. When I got to her, I noticed that Rudy was right behind me. Thank goodness we are both strong swimmers!

I saw her kicking under the water. At first she twisted away, but Rudy helped me pull her to the surface. She choked and struggled to breathe, but I held her tight and swam to safety. Everyone cheered as we got her safely up on the dock.

I think you are right, Grandma. I'm going to stop competing in swimming races. Instead, I'm going sign up for a water safety class so I can become a lifeguard.

Love,
Wayne

19

A **Circle the correct answer for each question.**

1. To what does Wayne compare himself in the June 18 letter?

a.

b.

c.

d.

2. What is the theme of this selection?

   a. Winning is everything.

   b. Everyone can do something well.

   c. There is always someone worse off than you.

   d. One good turn deserves another.

3. What was Grandma's first advice to Wayne?

   a. Keep practicing.   c. Play tennis.

   b. Stop racing.   d. Take lifesaving.

4. Why didn't Wayne win any races?

   a. He did not practice enough.

   b. He did not enter enough races.

   c. He raced against faster swimmers.

   d. He did not want to win enough.

5. Which phrase from the selection gives a clue to the meaning of *practice*?

   a. *following your advice*

   b. *swim laps over and over again*

   c. *is still clumsy*

   d. *is not improving*

6. How did being on the swimming team help Wayne?

   a. It helped him to win swimming and diving contests.

   b. It provided him with something to tell his grandmother.

   c. It made him strong enough to save a drowning child.

   d. It helped him make friends with his buddy Rudy.

B What class are you in? Are you a Tadpole, a Sardine, or a Dolphin? For the words in the list below, find synonyms (words that mean the same) in the box. Then write the synonyms next to the words. Next, see how many answers you got right. Finally, use your score to determine what class you are in.

advise	clumsy	trophies
surface	champion	wilted
compete	harbor	jealous
struggle	toured	toddled

1. port _____

2. bumbling _____

3. prizes _____

4. top _____

5. winner _____

6. drooped _____

7. battle _____

8. guide _____

9. visited _____

10. wobbled _____

Scores

Answers Correct	Class
1–2 . . . . .Tadpole
3–4 . . . . Minnow
5–6 . . . . .Sardine
7–8 . . . . .Codfish
9–10 .Dolphin

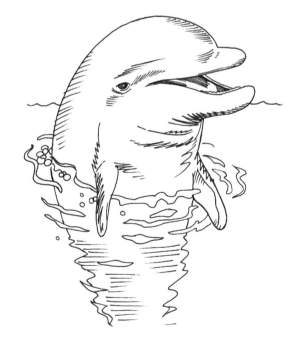

21

Selection 4: Paired

Young Heroes: Local Boys Save Toddler
By Chris Boyd
HMH Times

OCTOBER 30 PORT CITY GAZETTE   Denise Bell, 2, of Port City, was rescued from the waters of Port City Harbor by two quick-acting young boys on the afternoon of October 29. Wayne Hill and Rudy Gómez were on a class field trip to see the sailing ships when 11-year-old Wayne saw Denise Bell tumble from the deck of her parent's houseboat.

"I didn't think about it," Wayne explained. "I just dove in the water and swam to the little girl."

Rudy Gómez added, "Our teacher made me Wayne's buddy for the field trip. Wherever he went, I had to go. He jumped in the water, and I didn't think about it. I just went right in behind him."

Denise Bell's parents were trying to dock their houseboat when the accident occurred. They were distracted by the challenges of docking in the crowded harbor.

"We only took our eyes off Denise for a minute," Mrs. Bell said. "She was in the water before I had a chance to react. I am thankful for the quick actions of these two boys."

Though neither boy has had lifesaving training, both are strong swimmers. On October 29, their swimming lessons paid off. Port City and the Bell family are proud of the two young boys. In honor of their heroic actions, the boys will ride on a float in the Thanksgiving Day Parade. In addition, the Bell family is making a donation to the county children's swim program.

Conrad Bell, the father of Denise, will be adding a railing around the open end of the family's houseboat to prevent future accidents.

Ⓐ Circle the correct answer for each question.

    1. According to selections 3 and 4, who dove in the water first?

       a. Rudy   **c.** Mr. Clemente

       b. Wayne   **d.** Mrs. Bell

22

2. According to selections 3 and 4, how did Denise get in the water?

    a. She jumped in to get closer to the sailing ships.

    b. She was alone on the boat when it was moving.

    c. She fell in when she was startled by Wayne yelling at her.

    d. She fell in when her parents were distracted docking the boat.

3. Which sentence tells why Rudy jumped into the water?

    a. *Rudy wants me to be like him and not enter the swim races...*

    b. *When I got to her, I noticed that Rudy was right behind me.*

    c. *At first she twisted away, but Rudy helped me pull her to the surface.*

    d. *Wherever he went, I had to go.*

4. According to selections 3 and 4, what skill did Wayne have that helped him on October 29?

    a. He was a strong swimmer.

    b. He was alert to his surroundings.

    c. He had experience sailing.

    d. He followed the field trip rules.

5. According to selections 3 and 4, what will happen in the future? Circle all answers that are true.

    a. Rudy will join the swimming team with Wayne.

    b. Wayne will work to become a lifeguard.

    c. Mr. Bell will make his houseboat safer.

    d. Wayne's coach will give him a medal.

    e. Rudy and Wayne will be honored on Thanksgiving.

    f. Wayne and Rudy will teach Denise how to swim.

6. Which selection has a third-person narrator?

    a. Selection 3

    b. Selection 4

7. How can you tell the selection is narrated in the third person?

    a. the use of pronouns *I* and *my*

    b. the use of pronouns *he* and *they*

Selection 4: Paired
Core Skills Reading Comprehension, Grade 4

B Write the following facts from selections 3 and 4 in the correct column on the graphic organizer.

> Mr. and Mrs. Bell stopped watching Denise for a minute.
>
> Wayne dove in the water to save Denise from drowning.
>
> Wayne swims laps in the pool every morning.
>
> Wayne and Rudy's class takes a tour of sailing ships.
>
> Wayne and Rudy use their strong swimming skills.

In Selection 3	In Selection 4	In Both Selections

C The topic sentence of a paragraph is not always the first sentence. It can be anywhere in a paragraph. Read each paragraph below. Then find and underline the topic sentence.

1.   Rita Chapa practices at the indoor pool every day after school. She reads books about swimming to improve her strokes. For two years, she has won the city backstroke championship. In races, her team has always finished in first place. Rita is the best swimmer on the team.

2.   The Greeks and Romans taught their children to swim early in life. The sport helped them to develop strong, healthy bodies. These ancient people believed that swimming was a very important exercise. Being able to swim prepared the soldiers for land and sea battles.

3.   During the Middle Ages, people in Europe were afraid to swim. It was said that going into the water helped spread sicknesses. People seldom took baths either. It was not until 1850 that people found that they could put themselves into water without becoming ill.

4.   Because he had lost his math homework, Aiden was kept after school. That made him an hour late for swimming practice. By the time Aiden arrived at the pool, his friend Josiah had gone home. "This is certainly not my lucky day!" said Aiden. Just as he said that, he caught his favorite T-shirt on a nail sticking out of the fence. His shirt tore on the nail.

5.   Houseboats are floating houses. Unlike other boats, houseboats have flat bottoms. To give enough living space, they have to be wider than other boats. Because of that, they aren't as safe in the water as regular boats are. Houseboats are much slower. They are more difficult to steer, so it takes longer to get them away from dangerous places. Houseboats should always stay in safe, calm waters. These are the main differences between houseboats and other types of boats.

D **Now it is your turn to be the writer. Below are three topic sentences. Write four details for each topic sentence. Remember, all the details must refer to the topic sentence.**

1. Yesterday was not my lucky day.

_____

_____

_____

_____

_____

25

2. Now I use the water safety rules every time I go swimming.

_____

_____

_____

_____

3. I'll never forget my first day in swimming class.

_____

_____

_____

_____

_____

E **The following paragraphs have one or more sentences that do not fit the topic. Draw a line through any sentence that does not refer to the topic sentence.**

1. Heroes are not always people. Sometimes animals can be heroes. A woman fell from a boat into deep water. The woman teaches in my school. While she was trying to swim back to the boat, her leg began to hurt badly. She started to sink. Suddenly a dolphin appeared. It kept her at the top of the water. A dolphin is not really a fish. With its bottlenose, it pushed her along to land.

2. It is not necessary to be a champion to enjoy sports. People swim, bowl, dive, run, jog, play ball, and ride bikes just for fun. People like to go to the library. Strong, healthy athletes stay in shape and feel better. Some people have trouble singing. Girls and boys who play on teams learn that it is okay to win or lose. Just enjoying sports for fun gives people exercise and a good feeling about themselves.

Selection 5

My name is Donna. I don't mean to brag, but I am a good detective.

Last autumn my brother Nicky, my parents, and I moved into a large apartment house. Nicky and I have two friends across the hall named Liz and Glenn. In the apartment next door lives a man, Captain Field. He is very friendly to kids and never yells at us. He has collected many interesting things that he shows to us. He even lets us touch them. He often takes Liz, Glenn, Nicky, and me with him when he drives around the city to look for more things to collect.

Glenn once asked, "Did you get all your treasures in this city, Captain?"

"No," answered the captain. "I was in the army. I traveled to many strange places where I found things you never see around here."

One day, a man dropped in to see Captain Field.

"Mr. Kimble!" the captain cried out. "What a nice surprise to see you again!"

"I just flew in from Japan," said Mr. Kimble. "I need a place to stay for a few days."

Mr. Kimble stayed with the captain for a week. He was a traveler, too, and had many interesting stories to tell. My friends and I listened to him for hours at a time.

On the last day of the visit, Mr. Kimble and the captain asked our parents if Nicky, Glen, Liz, and I could come and look at the captain's jewels. It seemed a good idea since it was a stormy day, and we could not play outdoors.

The captain kept the jewels in a tiny room that had no windows. The door to that room was always kept locked. The captain unlocked the door and let us in. We were excited to see three glass cases of beautiful jewels.

It was almost time for us to go when the captain said, "Last of all, I want to show you my greatest treasure."

He took out a tiny bag and showed us six large, shining diamonds. Just then the storm outside got stronger. Thunder boomed and all the lights went out! The room became as black as ink.

"Stand still, everybody!" shouted Nicky. "I'll run to the kitchen and get the candles."

The captain said, "I'll feel around for a flashlight."

I stood quietly in one spot because I couldn't see a thing. I heard the others bumping into things as they tried to walk in the darkness. I heard Nicky yell as he ran into a wall while trying to find the door. He kept talking to himself, and I decided to follow his voice.

"I'm in the kitchen because I can feel the sink," Nicky said. I went nearer to his voice. "I found the candles under the sink," Nicky said, "but where are the matches?"

We felt around under the sink. Suddenly I heard a small bang. I knew it was a noise I often heard at home. But in the darkness, I could not remember what made that small bang.

"Who is in the kitchen with Nicky and me?" I called out.

It was very strange that no one answered. But I felt someone brush past me and slip out of the kitchen and into the hall.

About two minutes later Liz yelled, "The captain found two flashlights!"

Then a beam of light came into the kitchen. The captain and Liz flashed the light on Nicky and me. With this light we found some matches and lit the candles. Each of us had a light as we went back down the hall. Liz went to find Glenn who had gone into the bedroom by mistake in the dark. The rest of us went back to the treasure room and found Mr. Kimble still sitting there.

"I just can't stand to creep around in the dark," he said.

The captain looked for his diamonds with the flashlight. They were gone!

Just then the lights came on again. The captain searched the whole apartment. We felt terrible because the captain was so upset. I hoped that Liz and Glenn and Mr. Kimble had not stolen the diamonds because they were all my friends. I knew Nicky and I had not taken them. Though the captain searched us and searched the apartment, he did not find the diamonds anywhere. We took everything out of our pockets. No one had the diamonds.

"I must think like a detective," I thought. "No one opened the door to leave the apartment while the lights were out. The diamonds must still be here somewhere."

The next day Mr. Kimble was ready to leave. My friends and I came to tell him good-bye. It was not a happy time because everyone was thinking, "Who stole the diamonds?"

The captain was going to drive Mr. Kimble to the airport.

Mr. Kimble said, "I think I'll fix a thermos of cold lemonade to take with me. I'll get some ice cubes now."

He opened the freezer door. Then I remembered! This was the sound I had heard in the kitchen in the dark. I watched Mr. Kimble put the ice cubes into his thermos.

"Just a minute!" I said, even though I was shaking with fear. "Mr. Kimble, I think you should return the captain's diamonds!"

"What do you mean?" snapped Mr. Kimble. "You'd better watch that sharp tongue of yours. It could get you into trouble!"

"Yes, what do you mean?" asked the captain. "Don't speak to Mr. Kimble like that!"

"I heard the freezer door open last night," I told everyone. "Someone was hiding the diamonds in there because no one took out any food in the dark."

"Are you saying I did it?" asked Mr. Kimble in a cold voice. "Can you prove it?"

Then I really was upset. Could I prove it? I had to think quickly.

"The diamonds are the same color as ice!" I shouted. "The person who stole the diamonds stuck them in an ice cube tray where they would look just like ice."

I took the thermos and carefully put all the ice cubes into a dish. When the ice cubes had melted, six shining diamonds lay in the dish of water.

"They were so beautiful," said Mr. Kimble, "that I just had to have them."

"Donna, I have met many people in my travels, but you are the best detective in the world!" said the captain. "Thank you!"

"It was easy," I said, "because we detectives think!"

Ⓐ Underline the right answer to each question.

1. Why did the children like to visit Captain Field?

   a. He gave them many treasures.

   b. He was their parents' friend.

   c. He was their teacher in school.

   d. He got along well with children.

2. When did the captain collect most of his treasures?

   a. when he took drives around the city

   b. when he visited his friends

   c. when he traveled with the army

   d. in the autumn of the year

3. What happened just before the lights went out?

   a. The captain unlocked the treasure room.

   b. The children started to go home.

   c. The thunder boomed loudly.

   d. The captain said, "I'll feel around for a flashlight."

4. How did Nicky know that he was in the kitchen?

   a. He felt the sink.

   b. He followed Mr. Kimble in there.

   c. He slipped on an ice cube.

   d. He saw the freezer door.

5. What gave Donna the idea that the diamonds were still in the captain's apartment?

   a. She felt cold when someone passed by her.

   b. Everyone was in the apartment when the lights came on.

   c. Only the captain could open the front door.

   d. The doors and windows were kept locked.

6. Who turned out the lights?

    a. Liz and Glen   **c.** Captain Field

    b. nobody   **d.** Mr. Kimble

7. What does it mean to have a "sharp tongue"?

    a. The person says loud things.

    b. The person says mean things.

    c. The person gives wrong answers.

    d. The person's tongue has a point on it.

8. Why did Mr. Kimble put the diamonds in ice cube trays?

    a. Diamonds melt if they are not kept cold enough.

    b. The ice cube tray was next to his chair.

    c. The captain never used any ice cubes.

    d. Diamonds are the same color as ice.

9. What happened first after Donna heard a strange noise?

    a. Donna followed Nicky into the kitchen.

    b. Nicky bumped into the sink.

    c. The captain came in with a flashlight.

    d. Someone slipped out of the kitchen.

10. How did Donna prove that Mr. Kimble took the diamonds?

    a. She found the diamonds in Mr. Kimble's ice cubes.

    b. She took a picture of him opening the freezer.

    c. She found diamonds in his coat pocket.

    d. He was in the treasure room when the lights came on.

11. What is the best title for this selection?

    a. Nicky's Lucky Guess

    b. Detectives Must Think

    c. A Visitor Needs Help

    d. Nicky and Donna Move

B Draw lines to match these words and meanings.

1. someone who finds missing things   brag

2. a place to live in a larger building   autumn

3. important person in the army   apartment

4. to say nice things about yourself   lemonade

5. gathered together in one place   captain

6. a small light to hold in your hand   detective

7. the fall season of the year   collected

8. a hard stone that looks like ice   thermos

9. took something without the right to   stole

10. container that keeps drinks hot or cold   flashlight

11. a group of people who are ready to fight
    in times of war   diamond

                                                                                   jewels

12. things people wear that are made from pretty stones   army

C Underline the right answer to each question.

1. Liz and Nicky moved in the autumn. Which is the date that they might
   have moved?

   a. April 25   **b.** February 7   **c.** November 10

2. They moved into a large apartment house. What do we know about where
   they lived?

   a. Each family had its own large house.

   b. Many families lived in one building.

   c. Several families lived in one room.

3. When there is no light, people cannot see. How might they tell what is around
   them in the dark?

   a. by hearing, touching, smelling, and tasting

   b. by touching, hearing, looking, and smelling

   c. by smelling, touching, looking, tasting, and hearing

Name _____ Date _____

D The point of view of a text tells who the narrator is. In first-person point of view, the narrator is a character in the selection. The author uses the pronouns *I, me, my,* and *we.* Things in the selection are described from that character's point of view. In third-person point of view, the narrator is an observer. The author uses the pronouns *he, she,* and *they.* Things in the selection are described as if being watched from the outside.

Read each quote. Write *first person* or *third person* to tell the point of view.

Selection	Quote	First Person or Third Person?
1	She flew up in the air and startled the monkey, who had just lit the candles on his friend's birthday cake.	
2	Chipmunk ran as fast as he could back to the safety of his hole in the ground.	
3	After we toured the ship from Norway, we were lined up on the dock while Mr. Clemente made sure we were in pairs. (I was paired with my buddy Rudy Gómez, of course.)	
4	Denise Bell's parents were trying to dock their houseboat when the accident occurred. They were distracted by the challenges of docking in the crowded harbor.	
5	Last autumn my brother Nicky, my parents, and I moved into a large apartment house.	

Now, go back and underline the clues in each quote that tell you whether the selection is written with a first-person narrator or a third-person narrator.

E **Can you think like a detective? Read the clues. Then circle the right answer.**

Mr. Tanaka had twenty large cans of paint. He asked Aiden to stack the cans in four piles. Each pile had to have the same number of cans. Aiden finished in a few minutes.

1. What do we know about the paint cans?
   a. Mr. Tanaka has more paint cans since Aiden stacked them.
   b. Mr. Tanaka has the same number of cans as before.
   c. Mr. Tanaka does not have as many cans now.

2. How many cans of paint did Aiden put in each pile?
   a. four   b. five   c. six   d. seven   e. eight

Three children were saving money to buy Dad a new wallet for his birthday. Diego had saved four dollars. Camila had saved five dollars. Martín had saved two dollars.

3. Who had saved the most money so far?
   a. Camila   b. Martín   c. Diego

4. Who had saved less money than any of the others?
   a. Camila   b. Diego   c. Martín

5. How much money had the children saved together?
   a. six dollars   c. eleven dollars
   b. ten dollars   d. twelve dollars

6. The wallet they wanted to buy cost fifteen dollars. What do you know?
   a. They will need more money to buy this wallet.
   b. They will have money left over after they buy it.
   c. They have just enough money to buy it.

7. How much more money will they need to save?
   a. three dollars
   b. two dollars
   c. one dollar
   d. four dollars
   e. none

The Oaktown School is different from many other schools. Children there go to school every month of the year. Every month the children get one week off from school.

8. How many months of the year do children go to school in Oaktown?

   a. ten   **b.** nine   **c.** twelve   **d.** fifteen

9. How many weeks of the year are the children off from school in Oaktown?

   a. 0   **b.** 6   **c.** 10   **d.** 11   **e.** 12

10. Find out how many days you are off from school this year. Then change the number of days to weeks. Count five school days as a week. What do you know about your school?

   a. You have more time off than the children in Oaktown.

   b. You do not have as much time off as the children in Oaktown.

   c. You have the same number of weeks off as the children in Oaktown.

Tai took a small bag of nuts to the park. There were twenty nuts in the bag. He fed eight nuts to a squirrel. He gave nine nuts to a chipmunk. Tai ate the rest of the nuts.

11. What do we know about the bag now?

   a. Now there are some nuts left in it.

   b. Now there are many nuts in it.

   c. Now the bag is empty.

12. How many nuts did Tai feed to the animals?

   a. 0   **b.** 7   **c.** 9   **d.** 17   **e.** 19

13. How many nuts did Tai eat?

   a. 0   **b.** 3   **c.** 5   **d.** 13   **e.** 15

14. How many nuts were in the bag when Tai left the park?

   a. 0   **b.** 2   **c.** 4   **d.** 6   **e.** 8

Name _____ Date _____

Selection 6

"This is not my idea of fun," grumbled Kayla.

It was a chilly evening in February. Kayla Watts was talking to her twin brother Lamark. They were working in their father's antique store. Mr. Watts had needed their help to unpack a huge box marked FRAGILE.

Their father said, "I'm sorry, children. The box was delivered at closing time. It must be unpacked in time for the sale tomorrow."

At last the box was open. Mr. Watts carefully lifted the soft packing. It had protected the antiques on their long trip to his shop. Antiques are old things that were used by people long ago. Mr. Watts sold antiques in his shop.

The twins were not always interested in old plates, paintings, and fans. They disliked having to be so careful about handling them. But they knew it was important not to crack or break the valuable objects.

"This time we have some china cats," announced Mr. Watts. He unwrapped one.

"It's cute," said the twins together.

Quickly, all three unpacked more china cats. Suddenly they stopped! From the bottom of the carton came a strange moan.

"One of the china cats is mewing," said Lamark.

Now their father's fingers flew, pulling out everything.

Mr. Watts piled antiques on a table. He gently tipped the box over on its side. Out staggered a weak, skinny cat. It stumbled and fell flat on its face.

"This is strange!" said Mr. Watts. "This shipment took two days to reach here from London! How did this poor cat make it through the trip on a plane and in a truck?"

The children held the cat. They felt sorry for it. Mr. Watts got out his phone. He used a search engine to look up "Veterinarians." Then he tried one number after another, trying to find an animal doctor who worked late in the evening. He had no luck.

Kayla filled an antique dish with water. Lamark put it by the cat's mouth. The cat started to lick the water, but it stopped and looked around in fear. Lamark gave the cat gentle pets on the head and put drops of water on his fingers. Slowly the animal licked a few drops. The cat mewed loudly.

"I think he's hungry," Lamark said.

Mr. Watts wrapped the cat in a towel, and they took the cat to the car. On their way home, they passed a food store.

"Please run in and buy some cans of cat food." Mr. Watts handed Lamark some money.

When they got home, they ran into the house. All of them tried to explain about the cat to Mom. She thought of using an eyedropper to feed the animal. From it, she dripped warm water into the cat's mouth. Then she put a tiny bit of cat food on its tongue. The cat gulped it down.

"I thought the cat was hungry! He's been on a long trip!" Lamark said.

Kayla put a spoonful of food in a small dish and the cat began to eat on its own.

Dad took an antique basket and filled it with pillows. Lamark gently placed the cat in it. The animal soon fell asleep.

The next day, Mrs. Watts told the veterinarian what had happened.

"The cat was in a box of china from England. The carton traveled by plane across the Atlantic Ocean. The box was unloaded at the airport and came by truck to our shop here in Tarrytown, New York. That cat traveled over 3,400 miles!"

"This cat is like Jason!" Lamark said.

"Who is Jason?" asked Kayla.

Lamark explained, "I just read the myth about Jason. He was brave and led adventurers called Argonauts across many seas. This cat was brave and crossed an ocean to arrive here." That was how the cat got his new name—Jason.

Jason continued to have a big appetite. Soon Jason became a spoiled animal. He didn't like to stay alone. One day, when the twins were at school, Jason sneaked out of the house. Somehow he found his way downtown to the antique shop. Mr. Watts found him lying quietly on the shelf with the china cats. After that, Jason went with Mr. Watts to the shop every day.

"Jason is more careful around the antiques than the twins are," said Mr. Watts. "He's never chipped a thing."

In August, Mr. Watts flew to London to buy more antiques for the shop. After picking out the things he wanted, he said as a joke, "You never charged us for that wonderful cat. We like him better than all the china cats put together."

The Englishman, Mr. Lake, looked puzzled. When Mr. Watts explained, Mr. Lake's mouth opened in amazement.

"It must be our company cat, Hudson!" he exclaimed. "We have searched everywhere. Everyone here misses him!"

Name _____ Date _____

Mr. Watts returned home with a letter for the twins.

---

23 Pear Street   London, England

Dear Kayla and Lamark,

  Thank you for taking such good care of our favorite cat. We miss Hudson
very much. If you can bring yourselves to part with him, we will give you a free
trip to London to bring Hudson back. Once you are here, we would like you to
be our guests for two weeks.

  Hudson was named after Henry Hudson, the British explorer who crossed
the Atlantic and traveled to learn about parts of America. It seems Hudson
the cat lived up to his name! Since you have taken such good care of Hudson
while he's been exploring America, he is partly yours.

  You must decide whether to keep him or bring him back to us in England.

                                                    Sincerely,
                                                    Alexander Lake

---

What would you do?

A   **Read these questions carefully. Then underline the correct answer for
each question.**

  1. What happened first in the selection?
       a. A carton arrived from London.
       b. Mr. Watts phoned veterinarians.
       c. Mom used an eyedropper to feed the cat.
       d. Lamark bought cat food.

  2. What happened last in the selection?
       a. Jason went to the antique shop.
       b. The twins heard a meow.
       c. The twins got a letter from England.
       d. Hudson got lost.

Selection 6
                                   Core Skills Reading Comprehension, Grade 4

3. When did Mr. Watts and the twins find Jason?

    a. early in the day   **c.** at noon

    b. late in the day   **d.** about midnight

4. Why might Jason the cat be described as an *argonaut*?

    a. He lived in the time of Roman myths.

    b. Lamark read about traveling cats in a story.

    c. He was an adventurer who traveled a long way.

    d. Like the Argonauts, Jason flew on a plane.

5. Why do you think the cat was in the carton?

    a. Mr. Lake sent the cat to the United States as a gift.

    b. The packers thought the cat was an antique.

    c. The cat crawled in, and the carton was closed before he could get out.

    d. The cat wanted a vacation in New York and crawled into the carton.

6. When was the cat found?

    a. in the summer   **c.** in the autumn

    b. in the spring   **d.** in the winter

7. When did Mr. Watts travel to England?

    a. in the fall   **c.** in the winter

    b. in the summer   **d.** in the spring

8. What did the selection show about the twins?

    a. They were selfish.

    b. They were helpful.

    c. They were careless.

    d. They were mean.

9. Which of these would be an antique?

    a. a coat from last year

    b. a new chair

    c. a picture your mother painted

    d. a table made in 1800

10. How long was Jason trapped in the carton?

    a. about two weeks   **c.** about two days

    b. about two months   **d.** about two hours

11. After Mr. Watts heard the meow, "his fingers flew" as he unpacked the carton. What does that mean?

    a. He waved his hands.

    b. His hands shook with fright.

    c. He worked very fast.

    d. He cut his fingers on broken china.

12. In the selection, what did Jason dislike the most?

    a. unpacking the china

    b. traveling to China

    c. eating canned cat food

    d. being alone in the house

13. What is the selection mainly about?

    a. a helpful veterinarian

    b. a trip on a truck

    c. a journey across an ocean

    d. a cat's strange adventure

14. What will Lamark and Kayla get if they decide to return the cat to England?

    a. a reward and another cat

    b. a journey to the Hudson River

    c. a free trip to London

    d. nothing at all

15. Write your prediction about what Lamark and Kayla will decide to do. Use one detail from the selection to explain your reasoning.

_____

_____

_____

Name _____ Date _____

Write the correct word to complete each sentence.

amazement	moan	antiques	veterinarian	sale	skinny	explain
grumble	objects	gentle	valuable	sail	weak	explore

1. An animal doctor is also called a _____.

2. Something that is worth much money is _____.

3. Old objects that were used long ago are called _____.

4. To tell how something works is to _____.

5. To feel that something is a big surprise is to feel _____.

6. To complain is to _____.

7. Things are also called _____.

8. To travel to a place to find out about it is to _____.

9. A quiet groan is a _____.

10. Objects with reduced prices are on _____.

11. One who is very thin is _____.

12. Something or someone that is not strong is _____.

13. A thing that is not rough is _____.

Name _____ Date _____

C To understand what you read, you must know the meaning of the details in the selection. The details tell you *where, when, who, what, why,* and *how* about the action. Put all the details together, and you get a better idea of what the author is telling you.

Read the following selections. If you understand the details, you will know what to do with the pictures. Follow the directions carefully.

1. Mr. Watts had five china dogs in the shop window. Three looked just alike, but two others had different details on them. Kayla and Lamark had a hard time finding the two that did not match. See if you can do it. Circle the two dogs that do not match the others.

 a.
 c.
 e.

 b.
 d.

2. The Watts family has a nice home. Their house is wide and low and has a chimney. They have bushes near the house, but they have no garage. Mark their home with an X.

 a.
 c.

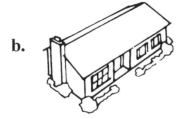 b.
 d.

Name _____   Date _____

3. One day Lamark and Kayla saw this sign in the window of the antique shop. Write complete sentences to answer these questions about the sign.

> **FREE SHOW!**   **BIG SALE!**
>
> ANTIQUE FAIR
>
> Friday, November 3
>
> 8:00–10:00 p.m.
>
> HARBOR HALL
>
> 123 Park Street
>
> Marble City

a. How much does it cost to see the show?

_____

b. Where will the antique fair be held?

_____

c. When will the fair be held?

_____

d. What can people do at the fair?

_____

4. Lamark and Kayla just got two books from the library. The books were written by their favorite authors. They know that one book will make them laugh. The other book will puzzle them. Circle the two books.

a. *THE MYSTERY OF THE ANTIQUE BOX* by Anna Hoodidit

b. *The Life of a Quarterback* by Michael Gridiron

c. *FISHING MADE EASY* by I.M.N. Angler

d. *Two Hundred Old Jokes* by Phil O'Chuckles

e. *ANTIQUE TOYS* by Susan Young Collector

5. Write answers to these questions about the books.

    a. What are the names of the authors of the two books Lamark and Kayla got from the library?

_____

    b. Which book might make them laugh? Write the title.

_____

    c. Which book might puzzle them? Write the title.

_____

    d. Which books might a sports fan read? Write the titles.

_____

    e. Who is the author of a book about old toys?

_____

D   **Read the prediction you wrote on page 42. Then read the following selection. Did your prediction come true or not? Answer the questions following the selection.**

    As Kayla and Lamark flew to London, they read a story. It was about a boy named Tom Tyler. About 175 years ago, little Tom Tyler lived on the streets of London. After his parents died, he was left alone. No one fed him. No one took care of him. He slept under bridges or in doorways of old buildings. He wore dirty rags and begged for food.

    In those days, there were many homeless children in London. Some stole food and coins. Others lived on scraps or money tossed to them by people passing by.

    Tom Tyler was skinny and short for his ten years. When someone threw coins to Tom, the other youngsters easily pushed him aside. If the grocer gave Tom an apple, the larger children grabbed it away from him.

    One chilly day, Tom stood near a group of workers. They were tearing down an old house. At last, one worker gave him a piece of bread and some meat. Tom was eager to eat the food. He did not watch his step. He stumbled into a hole. Then Tom rolled down a slope and hit an old stone wall.

    The food fell out of his hand. Tom searched through the loose dirt for it. How happy he was to find it! As he picked up the food, he saw ten round things lying in the dirt.

    Tom picked them up and brushed them off. They were coins. They were dull and had strange pictures on them.

    "Money is money," thought Tom. "I'll spend it." He ran to the baker to buy a sweet bun.

When he went to pay the clerk, she began to shout, "Wait, you thief! You gave me worthless trash!"

She threw the coins on the floor. With a broom, she chased Tom. A man standing nearby picked up the coins and rescued Tom.

"They're coins," panted Tom. "Why can't I spend them?"

The man looked closely at the coins. He said, "These are not English money. But they are worth much more. These are antique Roman coins. They are hundreds of years old."

The man helped Tom sell the antique coins. They earned Tom so much money that he never had to live on the streets again.

Kayla and Lamark were glad Tom found a kind and knowledgeable person to help him. Then they thought of Hudson the cat. They were also glad they were able to help Hudson.

1. Where does the selection Kayla and Lamark read take place?

_____

2. When does the selection Kayla and Lamark read take place? _____

_____

3. Why did Tom live on the streets? _____

_____

4. How did Tom get food? _____

_____

5. What did Tom find? _____

6. How did the man help Tom? _____

7. Who chased Tom with a broom? _____

8. Why was Tom unable to spend the coins? _____

9. How did Tom finally get enough money so he did not have to live on the streets?

_____

10. Why were Lamark and Kayla going to London? _____

_____

Now it is your turn to be a writer. First, write three details about Tom Tyler that describe his life on the streets. Then write three details about Hudson the cat that describe when he was found in the box. Write your details in complete sentences.

Tom Tyler

_____

_____

_____

_____

Hudson the Cat

_____

_____

_____

_____

F **Write the letter of the word on the right that matches the definition on the left.**

_____ **1.** without a home   **a.** rescue   **f.** knowledgeable

_____ **2.** having a lot of information   **b.** animal   **g.** dull

_____ **3.** to save from danger   **c.** homeless   **h.** lick

_____ **4.** not shiny   **d.** eyedropper   **i.** carton

_____ **5.** a box for shipping   **e.** antiques

_____ **6.** something a tongue does

_____ **7.** object that lets out a drip at a time

Name _____ Date _____

Skills Review: Selections 1–6

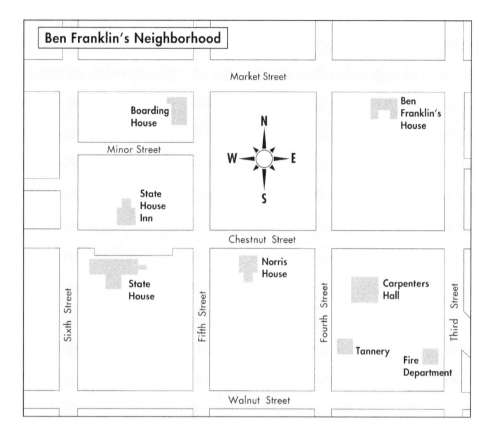

Ben Franklin's Neighborhood

Market Street

Boarding House

Minor Street

State House Inn

N
W — E
S

Ben Franklin's House

Chestnut Street

Sixth Street

State House

Fifth Street

Norris House

Fourth Street

Carpenters Hall

Tannery

Fire Department

Third Street

Walnut Street

0   100   200   300 feet
Scale 1 inch = 300 feet

A **Study the map above. Then answer the questions.**

1. What is west of Norris House? _____

2. What is the name of the street on which Ben Franklin's house is located?

   _____

3. Is Sixth Street east or west of Fifth Street? _____

4. Is State House Inn north or south of Boarding House? _____

5. What is the nearest building to the fire department? _____

6. Which is farther away from the fire department, State House or State House Inn?

   _____

7. What directions would you tell Ben Franklin if he wanted to walk to the Tannery?

   _____

8. What is most likely the name of the next street to the west of Sixth Street?

   _____

49

Skills Review: Selections 1–6
Core Skills Reading Comprehension, Grade 4

B **Read the following details. Use the details to follow the directions.**

1. Molly, Polly, and Dolly are triplets. Mom likes them to dress exactly alike. Molly and Dolly like to dress alike, but Polly does not. She wears something different so her friends can tell who she is. These pictures also give clues as to which triplet is Dolly. Dolly has lost something that the other two still have. Write the name of the correct triplet under each picture.

_____ _____ _____

Read the signs below. Note the details in each. Then answer the questions.

Sign 1	Sign 2
KEEP OUT! DANGER OF FALLING BRICKS! PIZZA PALACE closed for repairs *Will reopen March 18*	**CONTEST** **April 4–April 18** Win tickets to Carnival! Simply count the marbles in the jar! **Fill out an entry form today!**

2.

    a. Which sign tells about winning something? _____

    b. Which sign is a warning? _____

    c. Why is Pizza Palace closed? _____

    d. How long is the contest going to last? _____

    e. When will people be able to eat at Pizza Palace again? _____

    f. What must be done to enter the contest? _____

    _____

    g. What is the contest prize?_____

    h. How might someone get hurt? _____

C   **Choose the meaning of each underlined expression and write it on the line.**

Meanings	
a. by himself	**e.** all ears
b. start a conversation	**f.** say "no"
c. sick	**g.** look into
d. understood	

1. Ms. Acosta missed school today because she was feeling <u>under the weather</u>.

_____

2. Marcus rode the bus <u>on his own</u>.

_____

3. Alicia could not <u>turn it down</u>.

_____

4. To <u>break the ice</u> the new student smiled and shook my hand.

_____

5. I <u>saw the light</u> as I worked through my algebra homework.

_____

6. Be sure to <u>check out</u> the big sale at Sporting Goods Mart.

_____

D Most details tell something about a main idea. Details tell about or explain the main idea. Read the sentences carefully. Pick out the main idea and label it *M.I.* Label each supporting detail *D*.

1.

_____ a. One of the most important inventions of early people was the wheel.

_____ b. The wheel helped move heavy loads faster.

_____ c. Before the wheel, people had to drag heavy things.

_____ d. The wheel made it possible to take large objects from place to place faster and more easily.

_____ e. People were able to travel longer distances.

2.

_____ a. If a female bird is easily seen and killed by enemies, her eggs will never hatch.

_____ b. When females search for food for baby birds, their colors must blend into the trees and grasses.

_____ c. Female birds must blend into the shadows when sitting on nests to hatch eggs.

_____ d. Female birds are not brightly colored like male birds, so they can hide from enemies.

_____ e. Baby birds must depend on their mothers for most of their food.

3.

_____ **a.** Carrots and potatoes are the roots of plants.

_____ **b.** Lettuce and spinach are the leaves of plants.

_____ **c.** Vegetables come from different parts of plants.

_____ **d.** Celery comes from the stems of plants.

_____ **e.** When we eat peas, beans, and corn, we eat the seeds of plants.

E **The topic sentence of a paragraph may be anywhere in the paragraph. Search for the topic sentence in the following paragraph. Underline the topic sentence.**

One way monkeys use their paws is to gather and hold their food. Sometimes they use their paws to pick up sticks and banana peels and throw them at other animals. People like to watch a monkey looking through another monkey's fur. The monkey is using its paws to remove dead skin caught in the fur and to look for fleas. The paws make it easy for monkeys to climb trees and swing from branch to branch. Monkeys' paws are useful tools.

F **These paragraphs have one or more sentences that do not fit the topic. Draw a line through the sentences that do not refer to the topic sentence.**

1.   A gnome (pronounced nōm) is a creature in fairy tales. Nome is a city in the state of Alaska. The make-believe gnomes were said to look like tiny, old men. They had wrinkled skin and long beards. They were bent and stooped because they worked deep in the earth as miners. Moles also live deep in the earth and dig for food. Gnomes were said to find gold and jewels under the ground which they sometimes gave to kind princes and princesses. Anyone who did not please gnomes was soon repaid with spite and meanness.

2.   Birds can travel long distances when they migrate. Bobolinks travel as far as 12,500 miles to spend the winter in South America. The ruby-throated hummingbird travels without stopping 500 miles across the Gulf of Mexico. Columbus traveled many miles on his trips. When the weather becomes warm, the birds fly the same distance to go back north. A round trip for the Arctic tern is 44,000 miles. After their return to the north, robins begin to build nests.

G **Read the following two articles. Then underline the correct answer to each question.**

The male ostrich has black feathers on its body. Its small wings and its tail are covered with large, curly, white feathers. The ostrich's long, thin neck and legs do not have feathers. The skin of the ostrich may be pink or blue. Around its eyes are thick, black eyelashes. What a handsome, unusual bird the male ostrich is.

Nature has prepared the muskrat to spend most of its time in water. The muskrat's grayish brown fur is warm and waterproof. The webbed back feet act as paddles. Its long tail is used for steering through the water. Some say muskrats look like rats; some say they look like beavers. Muskrats are bigger than rats and smaller than beavers. What a cuddly animal the muskrat appears to be.

1. How are the two articles alike?

   a. They both tell about swimming animals.

   b. They both describe unusual birds.

   c. They both describe animals' appearances.

   d. They both tell how animals move.

2. What is the theme of the muskrat article?

   a. Small animals can move fast.

   b. An animal is just right for its habitat.

   c. Small animals can be strong.

   d. An animal can be unusual and handsome.

3. If the two articles were combined into one, what would be the best title for it?

   a. Two Unusual Animals

   b. Tall Birds

   c. What Does This Animal Remind You Of?

   d. How Animals Move

4. From the article, what conclusion can you draw about female ostriches?

   a. They have curly, white feathers.

   b. They must look different from male ostriches.

   c. They do not have feathers.

   d. They lay eggs and raise the young.

Selection 7

Mrs. Haywire was puzzled. She and Mr. Haywire just did not know what to give Hannah for a present. Hannah did not want a bike or skates or a camera. Two weeks before Hannah's birthday, Mrs. Haywire overhead her daughter speaking to her friend Jada.

Hannah said, "For my birthday, I wish someone would get me a puffin."

Mrs. Haywire giggled to herself. A puffin! Now she could make Hannah happy. She would surprise Hannah with the very thing she wanted.

There was only one problem. What in the world was a puffin?

Mrs. Haywire knew Hannah had the appetite of a starving shark. She always gobbled up everything on her plate. A puffin was probably some sort of dessert. Mrs. Haywire was a wonderful cook. She decided to make a puffin for Hannah.

And so Mrs. Haywire went to the store.
She walked to desserts on row number four.
The boxes and packages rose in tall stacks.
Surely a puffin was one of those snacks.

A brownie, a cookie, a cake, and a muffin.
But none of the boxes was mix-and-bake puffin.
At the front of the store, Mrs. Haywire asked, "Why?"
The manager said, "I don't have puffin to buy."

Mrs. Haywire inquired, "Then, where should I go?"
The manager said, "I really don't know."
So poor Mrs. Haywire, a frown on her face,
Got back in her car and drove place to place.

She asked for a puffin at each little shop.
By the end of the day she was ready to stop.
"Where is a puffin?" she asked with a cry.
A voice said, "Give the dictionary a try."

Name _____ Date _____

 Read the list below to learn how to use a dictionary.

Using the Dictionary

1. To help you find words easily and quickly, the words in a dictionary are arranged in **alphabetical order**.

2. The words in alphabetical order are in boldface type, or darker print. They are called **entry words**.

3. At the top of each page are two **guide words**. The first guide word is the first entry word on the page. The second guide word is the last entry word on the page.

4. All the entry words on the page, arranged in alphabetical order, come between the two guide words.

5. The entry words are broken into **syllables**. A syllable is a part of a word. (pud•dle)

6. Beside each entry word is its **pronunciation**. The pronunciation shows you how to say the word correctly. (pud′ əl)

Look at the guide words and page numbers below. Which page does Mrs. Haywire need to use to find out what a puffin is? Write the page number.

Mrs. Haywire needs page _____.

prove	101	prune		pudding	106	pug

pull	108	punch		punish	109	put

Find *puffin* on the dictionary page below. Help Mrs. Haywire learn what a puffin is.

---

pud•dle (pud′ əl) **1** *n*: a small pool of dirty water **2** *n*: a small pool of any liquid

puff (puf) **1** *v*: to breathe quickly **2** *n*: a short, quick blast

puf•fin (puf′ in) *n*: short-necked northern seabird

pull (pul) *v*: to move toward oneself

punch (punch) **1** *v*: to poke **2** *v*: to hit **3** *n*: a quick blow with the fist **4** *v*: to make a hole in

---

© Houghton Mifflin Harcourt Publishing Company

Selection 7
Core Skills Reading Comprehension, Grade 4

What did Mrs. Haywire learn from the dictionary?
"A puffin's a bird that lives by the sea.
No wonder those people looked strangely at me!
Next time I hear a word I don't know,
Straight to the dictionary I will go!"

B **Underline the correct answer for each question.**

1. Where did Mrs. Haywire go first to get a puffin?
   - **a.** to the dictionary   **c.** to the food store
   - **b.** to the zoo   **d.** to the Internet

2. What is the main idea of this selection?
   - **a.** how to pick out a good birthday gift
   - **b.** a trip to the grocery store
   - **c.** how to learn from pictures
   - **d.** when to use a dictionary

3. What is the best title for this selection?
   - **a.** Poems Are Fun
   - **b.** Hannah and Jada Plan a Party
   - **c.** Mrs. Haywire Learns Something
   - **d.** Mrs. Haywire, a Good Cook

4. Why did Mrs. Haywire use a dictionary?
   - **a.** She wanted to know the meaning of a word.
   - **b.** She wanted to find out where Jada lives.
   - **c.** She was looking for a puffin recipe.
   - **d.** It was the only book in her house.

5. What is a puffin?
   - **a.** a small bird that sings sweetly
   - **b.** a large bird that lives in the desert
   - **c.** a bird that lives near the ocean
   - **d.** a small pool of liquid

6. How many syllables are in the word *puffin*?

    a. one   **c.** three

    b. two   **d.** four

7. How is a poem different from a story, or prose?

    a. A poem has rhythm, meter, and sometimes rhymes.

    b. A poem has punctuation marks.

    c. A poem states a writer's opinion on a subject.

    d. A poem has lines of dialogue and stage directions.

8. What type of text is the quote from Mrs. Haywire at the top of page 57?

    a. drama   **c.** nonfiction

    b. poem   **d.** prose

 Use the following dictionary page to answer the questions.

---

sa • ble (sā′ bəl) *n*: a small animal valued for its dark, glossy fur

safe (sāf) **1** *adj*: free from danger **2** *n*: a place for keeping valuable things

sail (sāl) **1** *n*: a piece of cloth attached to a ship's mast so the wind will move the ship **2** *v*: to move on water

sale (sāl) **1** *n*: selling something for money **2** *n*: selling at lower prices than usual

salm • on (sam′ ən) *n*: a large, yellowish-pink fish with silvery scales

sand • pa • per (sand′ pā pər) **1** *n*: paper with a layer of sand glued on it **2** *v*: to smooth with this paper

saw (sô) **1** *n*: a tool for cutting that has a thin blade and sharp teeth on the edge **2** *v*: to cut with such a tool

scale (skāl) **1** *n*: a machine for weighing **2** *n*: plate covering fish and some animals

---

1. How many meanings are given for the word *saw*? _____

2. How many syllables are in the word *sandpaper*? _____

3. A *salmon* is a _____

_____

4. What is the meaning of *scale* as used in the sentence below?

> Mother removed the <u>scales</u> from the fish she caught.

_____

5. The fur of which animal was used in the fur trade? _____

6. Which word and meaning best describe the picture below?

GILBERT'S DEPARTMENT STORE
Winter Clearance

Sweatsuits $19.00 suit or $10.50 each piece	**Slouch socks** $3.50 a pair or 2 pairs for $5.00	**Felt Hats** $21.50 each Reg. $30.00	**Long Sleeve T-Shirts** $7.00 each Reg. $15.00 Many colors

_____

_____

7. Which meaning of *sail* is used in the sentence below?

> The girl raised the <u>sail</u> on the boat.

_____

8. Which two words are pronounced in the same way?

_____

9. What would you use to measure how much you weigh?

_____

10. What might a carpenter use to smooth a piece of wood?

_____

D **Predict what will happen to Hannah on her birthday.** *To predict* means "to tell what will happen in the future."

Make a ✓ by the ones that you can safely predict might happen on Hannah's birthday. Make an X by the ones that could not happen.

_____ **1.** Hannah's birthday cake will be shaped like a puffin.

_____ **2.** Mrs. Haywire will stuff and roast a puffin for Hannah's birthday dinner.

_____ **3.** Hannah will get a present of puffin eggs in a nest. She will sit on the eggs to hatch them.

_____ **4.** Jada will come to Hannah's party.

_____ **5.** Hannah will get gifts from her parents.

_____ **6.** Hannah will get a real puffin as a present.

_____ **7.** Hannah will not get a real puffin as a present.

_____ **8.** Puffins like cold weather, so Hannah will keep her puffin in the refrigerator.

_____ **9.** Hannah will keep her puffin in a bathtub filled with ice cubes.

_____ **10.** Hannah will get a framed poster of a puffin.

_____ **11.** Hannah will get a stuffed toy puffin.

_____ **12.** Hannah will get a book about puffins.

_____ **13.** Mr. Haywire will download a film about puffins to play at Hannah's party.

_____ **14.** Mrs. Haywire will go to Iceland and get Hannah a puffin.

_____ **15.** Hannah's parents will let her keep a family of puffins at home.

E Now it is your turn to be a writer. Find *scale*, *saw*, and *safe* in the dictionary on page 58. Write a complete sentence using each meaning of the word.

1. *scale* a. _____

   _____

   scale b. _____

   _____

2. *saw* a. _____

   _____

   saw b. _____

   _____

3. *safe* a. _____

   _____

   safe b. _____

   _____

F Write a word to complete each sentence.

strange	problem	giggle
manager	appetite	inquire

1. The _____ opened the story early.

2. The puffin has a _____ beak compared to many birds.

3. To ask a question is to _____.

4. The deep snow made it a _____ to get to school.

5. The funny story made the kids _____.

Selection 8

Snakes do not have hands. Feet and eyelids are also among their missing parts. The body parts snakes do have help them live in the animal world. Note their long, slender, slinky shapes. A snake has a head, two eyes, a mouth, a forked tongue, and colorful scales. The scales on a snake's stomach help it crawl fast. A snake's forked tongue helps it smell things. Snakes breathe air into their lungs. Some snakes have fangs. A snake's fangs are as sharp as thorns and are poisonous. They shoot venom into enemies that try to harm them. However, most snakes are not harmful!

Snakes are cold-blooded. This means that the temperature of their bodies is the same as the temperature of the air or water around them. If it is hot outdoors, a snake has a high temperature. If it is cold outdoors, a snake has a low temperature. In the winter, snakes hibernate to keep from freezing.

Snakes swallow their food whole. The prey a snake swallows is sometimes much larger than the snake. A snake's mouth opens very wide. Its jaws spread apart. Then, it gulps the food down, creating bulges in its body.

If all snakes like the same food, there would not be enough food for snakes to survive. Because of this, some snakes eat only eggs. Some snakes dine only on snails. Others enjoy meals of birds, rats, frogs, toads, or insects. Some snakes are even cannibals. A cannibal is one that eats its own kind—some snakes eat other snakes.

Snakes have many enemies. Humans are the worst. They kill snakes both for food and for their skin. Shoes, purses, wallets, belts, and jackets are made out of beautiful, scaly snake hide. Scientists have learned to make medicine from snake venom, too. Large birds are also snakes' enemies. They swoop down from the sky to grab a snake for lunch. Wild pigs trample on small snakes and then eat them. Cobras and king snakes sometimes make meals from small snakes, too.

Snakes are found in a variety of places. Some live in ponds and streams. Others may be seen on land and in gardens, woods, pastures, and trees. Most prefer damp, warm places such as swamps and jungles where they can be left alone.

Ⓐ **Underline the correct answer for each question.**

1. Which one of these sentence is *not true*?

   a. Snakes have no hands.

   b. Snakes close their eyes to sleep.

   c. Some snakes eat birds and toads.

   d. Some snakes have poisonous fangs.

2. What is the best summary of the fifth paragraph in the selection?

   a. Snakes can be used to make shoes, purses, wallets, belts, jackets, and medicine.

   b. Although snakes have many enemies, they hunt by swooping after birds, trampling on wild pigs, and eating cobras and king snakes.

   c. Some snakes are enemies of other snakes. Cobras and king snakes sometimes make meals from small snakes.

   d. Snakes have many enemies, including large birds, wild pigs, cobras, and king snakes, but human beings are the worst. Humans have many uses for both snake meat and snakeskin.

3. Why do some snakes avoid other snakes?

   a. They prefer the company of other animals.

   b. They are afraid of being eaten.

   c. They are staying away from humans.

   d. They are avoiding catching illnesses.

4. What does *cold-blooded* mean?

   a. The animal always has a cold internal temperature.

   b. An animal uses its body to change the outside temperature.

   c. The animal eats its own kind when the temperature is cold.

   d. An animal is the same temperature as the air or water around it.

5. Which sentence is true?

   a. When the air is hot, the snake is cold.

   b. All snakes are a threat to humans.

   c. Snakes use lungs to breathe.

   d. Snakes use gills to breathe underwater.

6. What is the best title for this selection?

    a. The Farmers' Best Friend

    b. Fear of Snakes

    c. How Snakes Protect Themselves

    d. Facts About Snakes

7. Why will you never see a snake with closed eyes?

    a. Snakes have no eyelids.

    b. A snake has only one eyelid.

    c. Snakes' eyelids are very heavy.

    d. Snakes must constantly watch for danger.

8. How do snakes eat their prey?

    a. They chew and swallow it.

    b. They trample it.

    c. They swallow it whole.

    d. They share it with wild pigs.

65

B **Use the following words to complete the crossword puzzle.**

bulge	forked
temperature	venom
fangs	lungs
jaws	trample
prey	swoop
swallow	cannibal

Across

1. two long sharp teeth
4. to step heavily on
5. in the shape of the letter *Y*
9. measurement that tells how hot or cold something is

Down

2. to make food go down the throat
3. one that eats its own kind
6. an animal hunted, killed, and eaten by another
7. organs used for breathing
8. snake poison

66

C Selection 8 has many important facts about snakes. To help remember them, make an outline. An outline has a special form.

- Each outline should have a title that tells what the whole selection is about.

- Each outline must have the main ideas in the selection. These are written with Roman numerals.

- Under each main idea are details that tell more about it. These are written with a capital letter in front of each detail.

First, look back at the selection about snakes. The selection has six paragraphs. Each paragraph has a main idea. Choose the main idea of paragraphs <u>1, 3, 4, 5, and 6. Skip paragraph 2.</u> Write each main idea beside a Roman numeral.

Main Ideas		
How a snake eats	Where snakes are found	Body parts of snakes
Enemies of snakes	What a snake eats	

Facts About Snakes

I. _____

    A. _____

    B. _____

    C. _____

    D. _____

    E. _____

III. _____

    A. _____

    B. _____

    C. _____

IV. _____

   A. _____

   B. _____

   C. _____

   D. _____

   E. _____

V. _____

   A. _____

   B. _____

   C. _____

   D. _____

VI. _____

   A. _____

   B. _____

   C. _____

   D. _____

   E. _____

   F. _____

Finally, find details for each main idea. Write them next to the capital letters under each main idea in the outline.

Details		
Gardens	Jaws that spread wide	Ponds
Rats	Woods	Scales
No eyelids or feet	Human beings	Large birds
Eggs	Bulges in body	Pigs
Jungles	Cold-blooded	Other snakes
Fangs	Toads	Eyelashes
Swallows prey whole	Swamps	Forked tongues
Lungs	Insects	Streams

Selection 8
Core Skills Reading Comprehension, Grade 4

D **Read the facts below. Then follow the directions to make an outline.**

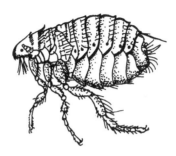

Fleas are dangerous, troublesome insects. They spread diseases from one animal to another. They carry sicknesses to humans, too. They make animals and people uncomfortable.

The tiny body of the flea is difficult to see. It is flat, short, and pale. Fleas have no wings. Their long, strong hind legs make them good jumpers. A flea has a long, sharp, sucking beak on its head.

Fleas are found in many places. They may be hidden in the fur of rats, rabbits, cats, and dogs. They can be found in the feathers of pigeons, chickens, and ducks. In places where animals sleep, fleas are found in rugs, furniture, grass, dust, and cracks in the floor.

All fleas eat the same thing. A flea uses its sharp beak to make a hole in the skin of people or animals. Then they suck the blood of their prey. Blood is the only food eaten by fleas.

Put the information in a shorter form by outlining it. Choose the main idea for each paragraph. Write each main idea by a Roman numeral. Be sure to title your outline.

Main Ideas	
How fleas eat	Why fleas are dangerous
Where fleas live	What fleas look like

Title: _____

I. _____

   A. _____

   B. _____

   C. _____

II. _____

    A. _____

    B. _____

    C. _____

    D. _____

III. _____

    A. _____

    B. _____

    C. _____

    D. _____

    E. _____

IV. _____

    A. _____

    B. _____

Next, find details for each main idea. Write the details next to the capital letters under each main idea.

Details	
No wings	Make people and animals uncomfortable
Cracks in floors	Strong hind legs for jumping
Suck blood of prey	Flat, short, pale
On animals' fur	Places animals sleep
Long, sharp, sucking beak	Make hole in skin of prey
Spread diseases to humans	In birds' feathers
Spread diseases to animals	Rugs and carpets

Selection 9

Pearls

A pearl begins its life as a speck of sand or as a very small sea animal. Either of these can be swept into an oyster's shell. The oyster cannot get rid of this unwelcome visitor. The gritty sand or the biting sea animal hurts the oyster.

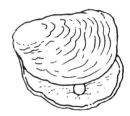

To protect itself, the oyster begins to cover the object with a layer of pearly material. After the object is completely covered, the oyster forms another layer over the first layer. It builds layer on top of layer until there is a round, shiny pearl inside the oyster shell.

Divers swim through cold ocean water to reach the oyster beds. Then they bring the oyster shells to the surface. After the oysters are washed, the shells are opened. The pearls are then removed.

The best pearls are used for necklaces. They are sold as jewelry.

Peanuts

This is a peanut plant. One day yellow buds on it open at sunrise. By noon, the blossoms are already dead. The bottom of each flower begins to grow, forming a "peg." This peg is really a stem.

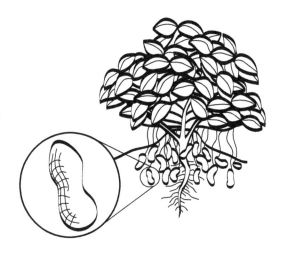

The peg, or stem, grows and begins to hang down to the ground. Then the peg pushes itself into the earth. The top of the peg has a little seed inside. As the stem goes deeper in the ground, the seed in the tip swells. It gets larger and larger until it becomes a peanut. Every flower grows into a peg. Every peg turns into a peanut.

The peanuts are picked by pulling each whole plant out of the ground. After the plant dries, the peanuts are removed.

Butterflies

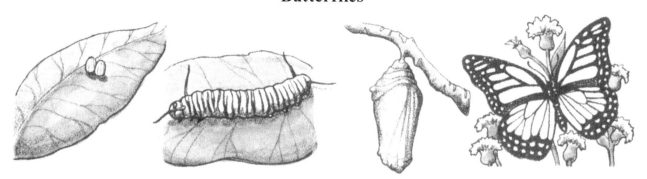

The female butterfly always lays her eggs on leaves. She picks the kind of leaves the larvae will feed on. Not all butterfly larvae eat the same kinds of plants. In a few days, the eggs begin to hatch. The larvae come out. Butterfly larvae are known as caterpillars.

The caterpillars are greedy little creatures. They eat leaves until they are fat, round, and ready to burst. They become too large for their skins and shed them four or five times. Still, they keep eating.

After a caterpillar gets its fifth skin, it begins to spin a silk thread and fastens itself to a twig or leaf.

Once it is tied tightly, the caterpillar spins a silky thread all around its body. When it is completely covered, it is inside a cocoon. This is the pupa. The pupa inside the cocoon changes its appearance. When the cocoon bursts open, a weak and wet butterfly comes out. Slowly, it fans its wings, dries out, gets strong, and flies away. It is hard to believe that the butterfly was once a crawling caterpillar and an ugly pupa.

Pens

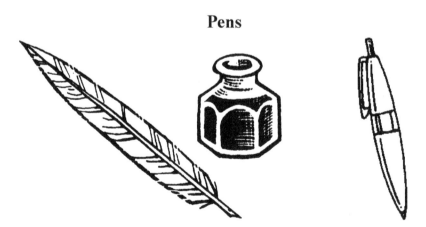

In ancient Rome, people used a pointed piece of bone or metal to write words on thin, waxed boards. Later, people wrote with hollow reeds. Hollow reeds are tall, stiff plant stems. People wrote on pieces of parchment (animal skins). Ink was placed inside the hollow stem to make marks when the reed was pushed down on the parchment.

A few hundred years later, someone discovered that the long wing feathers of a swan or a goose made good pens. The end of the feather was sharpened into a point. These pens were called quills. Quills were used for many years.

To write on paper, it was necessary to add steel tips to the quills. In 1884, the first fountain pen was invented. These pens were filled with ink and could be used until the ink ran out. Then the pen could be refilled and used again.

Fountain pens were mainly used until 1944. Then ballpoint pens were developed. Many people today still use ballpoint pens. Felt-tipped pens were first made in 1951. In the 1980s, roller ball pens were developed that used a ball and ink to produce a smoother line than a ballpoint pen.

A **Underline the correct answer for each question.**

1. Where are pearls found?

   a. in plants   **c.** on parchment

   b. in pupas   **d.** in oceans

2. How are pearls and peanuts alike?

   a. how they form

   b. where they grow

   c. their yellow color

   d. how they are used

3. Which sentence tells you that peanuts grow underground?

   a. *By noon, the blossoms are already dead.*

   b. *Then the peg pushes itself into the earth.*

   c. *Every flower grows into a peg.*

   d. *After the plant dries, the peanuts are removed.*

4. What is a caterpillar?

   a. the egg   **c.** the larva

   b. the pupa   **d.** the adult

5. What structure did the author use in writing "Pens"?

   a. cause and effect   **c.** time order

   b. comparison   **d.** problem and solution

6. Which sentence is an opinion?

    a. The female butterfly lays eggs.

    b. A caterpillar will eat any leaf.

    c. The caterpillar is the most fascinating stage of a butterfly's life.

    d. Inside a cocoon, a pupa changes appearance to become a butterfly.

7. Where are the eggs of butterflies laid?

    a. on leaves   **c.** in flowers

    b. underground   **d.** in a cocoon

8. How are pearls started?

    a. with eggs laid by the oyster

    b. with a speck of sand

    c. with layers of sand

    d. by an illness

9. Why could a fountain pen be used for a long time?

    a. The ink gets used up.

    b. They were made of bone.

    c. They could be refilled.

    d. none of these

10. George Washington used a quill pen. With what was he writing?

    a. a roller   **c.** a large reed

    b. a goose feather   **d.** a ballpoint pen

11. What must be done to find pearls?

    a. dive into deep water to gather oysters

    b. pick oysters and wait for them to dry

    c. wait until the pupa bursts open

    d. gather cocoons from the ocean bottom

12. How are these four articles alike?

    a. They all tell about the lives of animals.

    b. They all tell about the work of scientists and inventors.

    c. They all tell how useful things were invented.

    d. They all tell the order in which things happen.

B Choose the correct word for each picture. Write it under the picture.

ballpoint pen	caterpillar	cocoon
felt-tipped pens	flower buds	ink
oyster	parchment	peanuts
pearls	peg	quill

1. _____ 4. _____ 7. _____

2. _____ 5. _____ 8. _____

3. _____ 6. _____ 9. _____

C Circle the correct word or phrase to complete each sentence.

1. The larva of the _____ is called a caterpillar.

    peanut   butterfly   pearl

2. The caterpillar changes into a _____.

    egg   quill   pupa

3. The bud flower of a peanut plant has a short _____.

          pearl   life   root

4. The covering around the pupa is called a _____.

          larva   parchment   cocoon

5. When the peanut flower dies, a small _____ begins to grow.

          peg   pearl   egg

6. An adult butterfly comes out of the _____.

          cocoon   reed   parchment

7. Writing paper made from animal skins is called _____.

          larva   parchment   quills

8. The peg becomes a _____.

          pupa   pearl   peanut

9. Peanuts grow _____.

          on stems above the ground

          on stems under the ground

          on leaves over the stems

10. The caterpillar sheds its _____.

          peg   cocoon   skin

11. A quill may come from a swan's _____.

          shell   ink   feather

12. An unwelcome visitor to an oyster in its shell might be a _____.

          sea animal   cocoon   peg

13. Another unwelcome visitor in an oyster shell might be a_____.

          speck of sand   oyster pupa   bird's feather

Name _____ Date _____

D Read the information below. Then answer the questions by writing the letter of the correct answer.

Everything's in Order

All things move in order from one stage to the next. You have grown from an infant to the young person you are now. You will go through more orderly stages until you become an adult.

Now see what you can remember about the stages of pearls, peanuts, butterflies, and pens. If you have forgotten, look back and skim the articles.

1. **a.** fountain pen

   b. quill with sharpened point

   c. hollow reed filled with ink

   d. roller ball pen

   Which came first? _____

   Which came second? _____

   Which came third? _____

   Which came last? _____

2. **a.** The caterpillar gets too fat for its skin.

   b. It spins a cocoon around itself.

   c. The eggs hatch.

   d. The hungry caterpillar stuffs itself.

   e. It gets a new skin.

   f. It spins a thread and fastens itself to a twig.

   Which comes first? _____

   Which comes second? _____

   Which comes third? _____

   Which comes fourth? _____

   Which comes fifth? _____

   Which comes sixth? _____

Selection 9
Core Skills Reading Comprehension, Grade 4

E **Underline two correct answers for each question.**

1. When do peanut flowers die?

    a. soon after sunset   **c.** in the morning

    b. before noon   **d.** just before midnight

2. When do pegs push into the ground?

    a. before the buds open

    b. after the pegs grow downward

    c. while the flowers are blooming

    d. after the flower blossoms die

3. When should peanuts be picked?

    a. before the flower bud opens

    b. after the plant is taken out of the ground

    c. after the plant and the peanuts have dried

    d. before the leaves grow

4. When did people begin to write on paper?

    a. after they used parchment

    b. before fountain pens were invented

    c. before they used parchment

    d. after ballpoint pens were invented

5. When were steel tips put on quill pens?

    a. before sharpened bones were used

    b. after felt-tipped pens were invented

    c. when writing paper came into use

    d. before fountain pens were invented

6. When do caterpillars shed their skin?

    a. after eating a lot and growing fat

    b. after hatching out of the eggs

    c. after going through the pupa stage

    d. while they are butterflies

Name _____ Date _____

F Read the stages in a butterfly's life. This text is out of order. Write the text in time order. The first sentence is done for you.

Stages of a Butterfly

The female butterfly lays eggs.

The caterpillar spins a cocoon.

The caterpillar sheds its skin.

The adult butterfly flies away.

The larva hatches from an egg.

The butterfly bursts out of its cocoon.

The pupa hangs quietly in the cocoon.

The greedy caterpillar eats and eats.

The butterfly dries out.

---

1. The female butterfly lays eggs.

2. _____

3. _____

4. _____

5. _____

6. _____

7. _____

8. _____

9. _____

© Houghton Mifflin Harcourt Publishing Company

Selection 10

Some Really Big Flowers

The size, height, and beauty of giant sunflowers attract many gardeners. Normally, giant sunflowers grow to be about 7 to 10 feet tall. Their flowers grow to be about 12 inches across. That's bigger than a basketball! Some people, though, try to grow their flowers even larger. In 1983, a woman in Canada grew a sunflower that was more than 32 inches across. That's as wide as an open umbrella! Then, in 1986, a person in the Netherlands grew a sunflower that was more than 25 feet tall. That's taller than many people's houses! These flowers both set world records. Growing sunflowers of your own can be a lot of fun, whether you set records or not.

Getting Started

Giant sunflowers are perfect for young gardeners. The seeds are large and easy to sow when the soil is loose. Plants shoot up quickly in hot weather and grow well in almost any type of soil. The amount of sunshine your flowers get will affect how they grow. For larger flowers, the side of a building or a fence facing south is a perfect place for planting. If you would like your plants to be very tall, try planting on the side facing north. The plants will grow taller from having to stretch to reach the morning sun.

Caring for Your Sunflowers

Once your baby plants start to sprout up out of the soil, water them just once a week. Give them a heavy soaking of water. That way the water will go deeper into the ground. Then the new roots will have to grow farther into the earth to get water. This makes the roots stronger. Strong roots are needed to hold up the tall, heavy sunflowers. Once your sunflowers grow bigger, start giving them less water more often. A light watering once every evening can work very well.

Did you know that plants need vitamins just like people do? The people who grow the biggest sunflowers use fertilizer in the soil. Different types of fertilizers help the sunflowers grow in different ways. Some fertilizers make them taller; others make them larger or healthier. You can find out more about fertilizers at a local garden store.

Planting Directions

Step 1
Choose a location that gets lots of sunshine.

Step 2
Wait until the last danger of frost is past before planting.

Step 3
Turn the soil until it is loose.

Step 4
Plant seeds about 1 inch deep.

Step 5
Pack soil firmly over seeds with your hand.

Step 6
Spray water gently over the seeds.

Step 7
Keep the soil extra moist for 3 to 7 days.

Not Just for Show

One of the best things about sunflowers is their delicious seeds. To save your giant sunflower seeds, cover each flower head with a paper bag. Do this as soon as the flowers begin to dry out. As the seeds ripen, this will protect them from hungry birds. You can roast your sunflower seeds in the oven or eat them straight off the dried flowers. Don't forget to save some seeds to plant in next year's garden!

Name _____ Date _____

Ⓐ **Underline the correct answer for each question.**

1. Read the sentence and the dictionary entry.

   The seeds are large and easy to <u>sow</u> when the soil is loose.

sow (sō) *v.* **1** to scatter seeds **2** to spread

   Which of the following words sounds like the dictionary entry word?

   a. saw   **c.** sore

   b. so   **d.** show

2. According to the diagram on page 81, what must a gardener do before planting sunflower seeds?

   a. Pack the soil firmly over the seeds.

   b. Keep the soil moist.

   c. Turn the soil until it is loose.

   d. Spray water gently over the seeds.

3. Choose the idea that completes the cause and effect chart.

Cause	Effect
A plant facing north stretches to reach the morning sun. →	

   a. The roots grow stronger.

   b. The flower grows larger.

   c. The seeds grow faster.

   d. The plant grows taller.

4. When the sunflower dies, why should you save some of the seeds rather than eat them all?

   a. to grow new sunflowers

   b. to feed the birds

   c. to set a world record

   d. to dry out the seeds

Selection 10
Core Skills Reading Comprehension, Grade 4

5. Which of these is an example of cause and effect from the selection?

    a. Normally, giant sunflowers grow to be about 7 to 10 feet tall. Their flowers grow to be about 12 inches across.

    b. Growing sunflowers of your own can be a lot of fun, whether you set records or not.

    c. Giant sunflowers are perfect for young gardeners. The seeds are large and easy to sow when the soil is loose.

    d. One of the best things about sunflowers is their delicious seeds.

6. Which sentence best tells the main idea of this selection?

    a. Some sunflowers are very large.

    b. Sunflowers are easy to grow.

    c. Plants need water and fertilizer.

    d. Sunflower seeds can be eaten.

7. What structure did the author use to write the diagram "Planting Directions"?

    a. cause and effect

    b. comparison

    c. time order

    d. problem and solution

8. What evidence does the author use to support the statement that the Canadian sunflower was unusually large?

    a. *Their flowers grow to be about 12 inches across.*

    b. *These flowers both set world records.*

    c. *The people who grow the biggest sunflowers use fertilizer in the soil.*

    d. *Wait until the last danger of frost is past before planting.*

B **Answer the questions using the encyclopedias.**

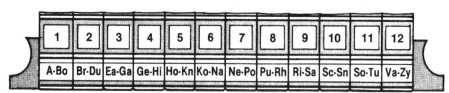

1	2	3	4	5	6	7	8	9	10	11	12
A-Bo	Br-Du	Ea-Ga	Ge-Hi	Ho-Kn	Ko-Na	Ne-Po	Pu-Rh	Ri-Sa	Sc-Sn	So-Tu	Va-Zy

1. Each book in a set of encyclopedias is called a volume. How many volumes are in the set above? _____

2. Topics beginning with certain letters can be found in Volume 8. Which beginning letters are found there? _____

3. Which beginning letters are found in the first volume? _____

4. What is the number of the first volume? _____

5. Which volume would you look in to find facts about sunflowers? _____

6. What beginning letters are on the volume you should look in? _____

7. You read that the sunflower is the state flower of Kansas. In which volume would you look to learn more about Kansas? _____

8. What beginning letters are on the volume you should look in to find information on Vincent Van Gogh, the artist who painted <u>Sunflowers</u>? _____

9. Write the number and the beginning letters of the volume you would look in to find these topics.

Topic	Number	Letters	Topic	Number	Letters
a. seeds	_____	_____	**e.** fertilizer	_____	_____
b. gardening	_____	_____	**f.** botany	_____	_____
c dirt	_____	_____	**g.** water cycle	_____	_____
d. frost	_____	_____	**h.** annuals	_____	_____

Use the Planting Directions diagram from the selection to answer the following questions. Underline the correct answer for each question.

1. In what season would it be best to plant sunflower seeds?
   a. winter
   b. spring
   c. summer
   d. fall

2. Which step in the diagram helped you answer question 1?
   a. Step 2
   b. Step 4
   c. Step 6
   d. Step 7

3. What is needed by sunflower seeds to grow?
   a. sunlight
   b. soil
   c. water
   d. all of the above

4. What should you do right after planting a seed?
   a. Make sure it is not too cold outside.
   b. Loosen up the soil around the seed.
   c. Cover the seed with soil.
   d. Choose a good location for the next seed.

Uses for Sunflowers

Sunflowers are pretty flowers and can add color to a garden. A vase of cut sunflowers can cheer up any room. Did you know that sunflowers also supply food?

Sunflowers are native to North America, and Native Americans were the first to use the seeds as a food source. They pounded the seeds into flour that was used to make cakes and bread. The seeds were also eaten as a snack. The flower petals were used to make yellow dyes.

Today the seeds are often sold roasted in the shell. People usually crack the striped shell with their teeth and then eat the little seed inside. Seeds can also be purchased already hulled. These are used for snacking or in cooking.

Another product of the sunflower seed is sunflower oil. Sunflower oil has a light taste and is a healthy cooking oil. It can be used in salad dressings or for frying.

D **Answer questions about "Some Really Big Flowers" and "Uses for Sunflowers."**

1. According to the two articles, what are two uses for sunflower seeds?
   a. to fry foods
   b. to eat as a snack
   c. to make fertilizer
   d. to make yellow dye
   e. to plant in the ground
   f. to scare away birds

2. Why would a grower of sunflowers want to protect the flowers from birds?
   a. The roots are weak, and the flowers can get knocked over.
   b. The seeds and flowers are poisonous to birds.
   c. They want to keep the birds from eating the seeds that people want.
   d. The presence of birds takes away from the color in the garden.

3. If the articles "Some Really Big Flowers" and "Uses for Sunflowers" were combined into one article, what would be the best title for it?
   a. Why I Like Sunflowers
   b. A Strange, Large Flower
   c. Cooking with Sunflower Seeds
   d. The How and Why of Growing Sunflowers

Selection 11

In 1900, in the small town of Dalton, there were two women with modern ideas. Mrs. Hyde, the mayor's wife, carried on a contest with Mrs. Rush, the banker's wife. They tried to see who could outdo the other in buying new things. Mrs. Rush put in the first telephone in town. Mrs. Hyde got the first upright piano. Mrs. Hyde bought the first camera. Then the Rushes got the first gramophone, an early record player. The contest between the two women went on.

In April, Mrs. Hyde startled the town by riding down Main Street in an automobile. It was the first seen in Dalton. The horses in the street bucked and kicked and ran away. Mrs. Rush turned emerald green with jealousy. But she was too scared to even think of riding in that noisy monster. What could she now do to outdo Mrs. Hyde?

Mrs. Rush thought about if for four weeks. Finally she had it! A bathtub with its own water heater was brought into the Rush house. This was a brave thing to do. The newspaper had just printed articles by famous doctors. They informed the people that too much bathing could cause many illnesses.

But Mrs. Rush was firm. The Hydes might ride in style, but her family would be the neatest and cleanest in town.

That was when Leonard Rush's troubles began! Up until then, Saturday night had been the worst time of the week. Then the whole family, even grumbling Grampa, bathed for Sunday. Now, every time Leonard got dirty hanging around the stable, he suffered for it. He was put into the tub and bathed. Once he had to take five baths in one week!

His sister Diana, who was sixteen, complained almost as much as Leonard did. She, too, was tubbed and scrubbed often.

One day in June, Leonard had his fourth bath in four days. Mrs. Rush looked him over.

"Are you sure the ring around your neck is gone?" she asked.

Leonard loudly replied,
"Yes, Mom! I'm clean and mean!
My skin's scrubbed raw!
Your bathtub should be against the law!"

After that, Father, Grampa, Diana, and Leonard Rush always said that rhyme when being forced to bathe.

Mrs. Hyde had a daughter, Polly, the same age as Diana. Diana was jealous when her friends spent time at Polly's house. They were hoping for rides in the automobile. In response, Diana and Leonard sang to their mother,
"Everyone is nice to Polly.
A ride in her auto is quite jolly.
But people look at us with pity.
We're the cleanest ones in the city!
Put wheels on the tub so we can ride,
And we'll be as popular as Polly Hyde!"

In August, the county judge's family held their yearly watermelon party. All the young folks in town were invited. There was ice cream, melons, games, and singing. At sunset, scrubbed and sparkling, Diana and Leonard walked up the hill to the judge's large house.

When Leonard and Diana entered the garden, their friends came to greet them. Leonard saw a crowd of young men by the swing. At parties the older boys always gathered around Elly Morgan. She was the prettiest girl in town.

Elly stepped away from the group of boys. Leonard noticed Elly's large, blue eyes and cloud of wavy hair, as golden as a field of ripe wheat. No one would have ever dreamed that Elly was the poorest, hardest-working girl in town. Since her father died, Elly worked on the farm with her mother. As the oldest of five girls, she also helped raise the younger kids. She was often unable to attend school for days at a time.

Now she pushed her way out of the crowd of admiring boys. She rushed over to Diana and Leonard.

"Diana, you are so lucky!" Elly exclaimed. "Imagine! You can take a bath without boiling water on the kitchen stove. You don't have to mop up the wet floor afterwards!"

"We don't think we're lucky," complained Diana. "I've been soaked so long that I feel like a wrinkled prune."

"It would be nice for me after working in the fields," sighed Elly. "And it would really help with bathing my two younger sisters."

Then Elly looked at Leonard. Never before had she even noticed him.

"Why, Len!" she cried. "How handsome you look! You're growing up into a very good-looking young man."

Leonard saw the older boys watching him jealously. He put on what he hoped was a charming smile. He said shyly, "Aw-w-w-w!"

"Would you like to come to our house sometime for a bath?" Diana asked Elly.

After that, Grampa could not believe his eyes when he saw his two grandchildren take baths *every day.* He sang,
"Look at that! One word from a girl
And Leonard's head is in a whirl!
He'll bathe and soak and clean and scrub
And never again grumble about that tub!"

By then, Mrs. Rush had all she could stand. She announced in a loud voice,
"Rhymes at breakfast! Rhymes at noon!
I don't like rhymes! Stop it soon!
The next one who dares to say a rhyme
Will not be eating at suppertime!"

Thanks to the contest between Mrs. Hyde and Mrs. Rush, the whole town started to try new inventions. Dalton soon became known as the cleanest and most modern town around.

Ⓐ **Underline the correct answer for each question.**

1. When does this selection take place?
   a. in the future
   b. in the past
   c. at this time
   d. twenty years ago

2. How often does the judge's family have the watermelon party?
   a. every six months
   b. every twelve years
   c. every winter
   d. every twelve months

3. Which of these would be the best title for this selection?
   a. A Bathtub on Wheels
   b. The Prettiest Girl in Town
   c. The First Horseless Carriage
   d. The Battle of the Bathtub

4. Which of these events happened first in the selection?
   a. Leonard suddenly liked to take baths.
   b. Mrs. Hyde got the first automobile in town.
   c. Mrs. Rush got the first telephone in town.
   d. Elly admired Leonard.

5. What color was Elly's hair?
   a. black   c. blonde
   b. red   d. gray

6. What happens last in the selection?
   a. Laws are passed against bathtubs.
   b. Fewer bathtubs are used in town.
   c. The town tries new inventions.
   d. The Rushes write a poetry book.

7. When did the first automobile appear in Dalton?

   a. spring

   b. summer

   c. fall

   d. winter

8. Mrs. Hyde and Mrs. Rush always tried to outdo one another. What does *outdo* mean?

   a. to do something outdoors

   b. to do better than

   c. to show off outdoors

   d. to get something out

9. What is this selection mainly about?

   a. how rhymes and poems are written

   b. how the automobile was invented

   c. people trying out new inventions

   d. people trying to invent something new

10. Which of these was a new invention in 1900?

    a. the stove

    b. the automobile

    c. the helicopter

    d. the wheel

11. Why do most people buy new inventions?

    a. to help the inventors

    b. to make work harder

    c. to waste money

    d. to make work easier and faster

12. What would most likely happen to Diana and Leonard if they rhymed again?

    a. They would have to prepare supper.

    b. They would have to wash dishes.

    c. They would have to miss a meal.

    d. They would have to clean out the tub.

13. Why did Leonard suddenly begin to take more baths?

    a. He liked to play in water.

    b. He wanted to invent something.

    c. He wanted to impress Elly.

    d. His grandfather made him do it.

B   **Choose a word to complete each sentence.**

monster	upright	emerald
informed	outdo	modern
judge	stable	dirty
mayor	gramophone	banker
suddenly	wrinkled	admire

1. To look at with pleasure is to _____.

2. Something that stands straight is _____.

3. A thing that is new or just invented is _____.

4. An _____ is a green jewel.

5. A _____ decides what is fair.

6. A person who handles money is a _____.

7. A place where horses are kept is a _____.

8. The head of a town or city is the _____.

9. A _____ is an imaginary and frightening thing.

10. An early record player was known as a _____.

11. To do better than is to _____.

12. Something that is not clean is _____.

13. To be told is to be _____.

C **Follow the directions carefully to answer each question.**

1. It took Mrs. Rush four weeks to decide how to outdo Mrs. Hyde. Underline all the answers that mean the same or almost the same as *four weeks*.

   a. seven days   **d.** a year

   b. about a month   **e.** twenty-eight days

   c. about two months   **f.** a season

2. Before getting the new bathtub, Leonard took a bath every Saturday. How often did Leonard bathe? Underline one answer.

   a. daily   **c.** monthly

   b. weekly   **d.** yearly

3. After Elly admired Leonard, how often did he bathe? Underline two answers.

   a. never again   **d.** five days a week

   b. daily   **e.** once a week

   c. monthly   **f.** seven days a week

4. Mrs. Hyde got her new box camera in February. What did she most likely photograph? Underline one answer.

   a. tulips in bloom   **c.** autumn leaves

   b. Diana sunbathing   **d.** outdoor winter scenes

5. Mrs. Rush got her gramophone a month after Mrs. Hyde got her camera. What month was it? Underline one answer.

   a. January

   b. March

   c. May

   d. September

6. The judge's family had a watermelon party every August. What is the most likely reason they had the party in August? Underline one answer.

   a. August is the judge's birthday month.

   b. That is when watermelons are ripe.

   c. August is the hottest month of the year.

   d. It kicks off the new school year.

7. Elly had to help her mother take corn to the market. She missed three weeks of school. How many school days did she miss? Underline one answer.

   a. fourteen days   **c.** twenty-one days

   b. fifteen days   **d.** thirty days

8. Grampa joined the children in chanting the rhyme about bathtubs being against the law. What does this tell you about Grampa? Underline one answer.

   a. He thought a once-a-week bath was plenty.

   b. He liked to smell good like Leonard.

   c. He bought the tub for the Rush family.

   d. He missed dinner for saying the rhyme.

9. Grampa caught a train at dawn. When did the train leave? Underline two answers.

   a. sundown

   b. sunrise

   c. late afternoon

   d. noon

   e. early morning

10. Grampa turned seventy years old in 1900. In what year was he born? Underline one answer.

    a. 1839   **c.** 1929

    b. 1830   **d.** 1930

11. Grampa came to the prairie in a covered wagon when he was a child. His parents left West Virginia in late February, 1840, and arrived in Dalton in ten months. In which month did they arrive in Dalton? Underline one answer.

    a. February   **c.** September

    b. June   **d.** December

12. Grampa waited at the train station for thirty minutes. Then the steam engine came puffing in. How long did Grampa wait? Underline one answer.

    a. two hours

    b. an hour

    c. a half-hour

    d. a minute

94

Name _____ Date _____

D Choose a word or words from the list below to complete each sentence. Some words will be used more than once.

one hour	one day
one week	one month
thirty	forty-two days
one minute	thirty-five days
one year	semester
six months	one second

1. Sixty seconds make _____.

2. Twenty-four hours make _____.

3. Three hundred sixty-five days make _____.

4. Sixty minutes are _____.

5. Twelve months are _____.

6. There may be thirty-one days in _____.

7. There may be twenty-eight days in _____.

8. Seven days make _____.

9. A half-year is _____.

10. Six weeks are _____.

11. A half-hour has _____ minutes.

12. A half-minute has _____ seconds.

Selection 12

Jasmine and Noah Dorn's father had lost his job in the big city where the Dorns had always lived. After a long search, Dad found a new job. The children's excitement over the good news turned to shock when they found out they would have to move to Oceanside, a very small town close to the seashore. Jasmine and Noah Dorn hated the idea of living in Oceanside.

Jasmine and Noah were upset. They could not give up their friends, their wonderful school, the library that had everything, and the sports they enjoyed.

Then their mother also found an excellent job in Oceanside. The Dorns had no choice. They had to move.

Mrs. Dorn tried to cheer up the children. "Guess what?" she said. "We found a big, beautiful house to rent. It's much bigger than the apartment we live in now. It's well kept, newly painted, and the rent is cheap."

Noah groaned. At the age of eleven, he knew when he was beaten. Cheap rent! There was no way his parents could turn down cheap rent.

Jasmine was nine. She did not know when to give up. "I despise the ocean!" she exclaimed. "I'm scared of those waves. The first time we went to Oceanside, I cut my foot on a broken shell on the sand. The seagulls are loud and messy. I won't go!"

"None of us wants to move, Jasmine, but we must," said Dad.

So here the Dorns were, stuck in a tiny village without shopping malls, movies, or all the places for sports and fun that they had in the big city. To make things worse, Jasmine and Noah faced a lot of teasing about their house.

It was called the Old Pinkney House. Everyone thought the house was unlucky because in 1885 the whole family that lived there had disappeared. They were never seen nor heard from again. Then in 1890, someone searching for clues on the Pinkneys' whereabouts also disappeared. From then on, only people who were new to Oceanside were willing to live in the Pinkney house at 743 Wendell Street.

"That's why the rent is so cheap," teased Amy Smith after school one day. "The owner wants to be sure the rent is paid before you disappear."

"Ha! Ha!" laughed Mamie James. "No use being friends with you two. As soon as I start liking you, you'll disappear."

Every week Don Aster said to Noah, "Don't waste time studying for the math test. You may go up in a puff of smoke before Friday."

The children complained to their parents and insisted they move, but got nowhere.

"Look what a nice place we're getting for next to nothing," said Dad.

Mom added, "Even when we had better jobs and made more money, we could not afford a house this big or beautiful. I am very happy here!"

That left Noah and Jasmine silent. Knowing how hard their parents worked, they could not complain again.

Noah and Jasmine did worry about their parents, though. Mr. and Mrs. Dorn worked long hours and often got home late. The children did not voice their fears to each other, but both were afraid that one evening their mother and father would not come home at all because they had disappeared.

"It's up to us to find out what happened to the Pinkneys," Noah told Jasmine.

That Saturday, they went to see Mr. López, the owner of the Oceanside newspaper. Mr. López got out copies of old newspapers from 1885. The children read the strange story of the Pinkneys' disappearance.

The men of the Pinkney family and many other men from Oceanside had been sailors. Many of the sailors were also smugglers, who used their boats to bring in goods from other places without paying taxes on the goods.

It was believed, the newspaper said, that the Pinkneys were telling the police about what the smugglers were doing. The smugglers had promised to get even with the Pinkneys. Shortly after that, the whole Pinkney family disappeared.

Five years later, in 1890, Zeke Little, the town handyman, told everyone that he knew what happened to the Pinkneys. "I'm checking it out," Zeke said. "I'll know by tomorrow, for sure."

But when tomorrow came, strangely enough, Zeke was gone. He, too, disappeared and was never seen again.

Mr. López told the children, "People have always said that the smugglers hid a wonderful treasure somewhere on Wendell Street. Many strangers have come searching for it, but nothing has ever been found. I think that the Pinkneys took the treasure with them when they left town."

"Treasure!" exclaimed Jasmine. "If we find the treasure, we can move back to the city!"

Mr. López and the children told Mr. and Mrs. Dorn about the treasure. They agreed to search the grounds around 743 Wendell Street. Some of the Dorns' neighbors joined them.

They searched the woods and the grounds near the house. They searched the stone path that went down to a little brook, and they searched the brook.

After they looked everywhere else, the searchers came to an old well in front of the house. No one used the well now, and there was a heavy wooden cover over it.

Mr. Dorn and two of the neighbors lifted off the wooden cover. Inside they discovered an old water bucket on a chain. Mr. Dorn tested the chain. Then he had the neighbors lower him into the well. He went all the way to the bottom, but he found nothing.

"That's enough searching for today," said Mr. Dorn. He thanked the neighbors for their help.

Later that evening, Noah whispered to Jasmine, "Let's go down into the basement. Maybe there are old papers or something that will help us."

They spent time deep in the basement looking through old books, pictures, and clothes for clues.

One day Jasmine discovered a faded little painting signed by Ann Pinkney, age seven. At the top was a title, "Our New House, 1875."

The house in the painting looked very different from the Dorns' house. There was no big porch, and there were hardly any trees and bushes around it. The brook was there, though, and so was the stone path.

"And here's the well," said Noah, putting his finger on it. "It's at the side of the house."

Suddenly something caught Jasmine's eye. "Look! Here is the front of the house," she exclaimed. "The well is on the wrong side!"

The children went outdoors to check. They stood in front of the house. The well their father had searched was on the left and closer to the brook. The well in the painting should have been on their right and near the side of the house. There was no well there. The ground was flat. A huge stone lay there.

"There was a well here," said Jasmine. "I know there was. The Pinkneys must have covered it with this big rock."

That night, the Dorns talked about the children's find. Mrs. Dorn said, "Maybe the well ran out of water. The Pinkneys dug a new well and covered up the old one. The smugglers remembered it and used the old dry well to hide some of their smuggled goods."

"That means the Pinkneys were smugglers, too," said Mrs. Dorn. "The well was on their land."

The Dorns worked with the Oceanside police and fire departments and their neighbors to uncover the old well and dig it out. Firefighters had the dangerous job of searching the dark hole. At the very bottom, they found some gold coins and a few old paper dollars. They also found two very old notes.

> To You Smugglers –
>
> So you want to get even with us! We'll show you! We have taken our part of the money. We are leaving the country. You will never see us again!
>
> John Pinkney

> To whoever finds this –
>
> I think the Pinkneys had a good idea. I'm taking the gold and jewelry and leaving. I'll be rich now!
>
> Zeke Little

"That's it," said Noah. "I guess there is no treasure left for us."

"Wait a minute," said one of the firefighters. "These may be worth money." She showed everyone about a dozen tin boxes of different sizes. In each box was a lovely seashell wrapped in silk.

"Those are rare shells!" exclaimed Mr. López. "Only a few have been found in the world. They are worth a lot of money."

"The town must decide who owns these things," said a police officer, "but you two kids may get a reward."

"We already have a reward," said Noah. "Everyone in town worked with us and helped us. It was fun! Now we don't want to move back to the city."

Mrs. Dorn agreed, "Friendship is a treasure."

A **Underline the correct answer to each question.**

1. What was the author's purpose in writing this selection?
   a. to tell a funny story
   b. to teach people how to work together
   c. to teach a lesson about smuggling
   d. to tell a story about strange events

2. What is the difference in the children's ages?
   a. Noah is two years younger.
   b. Noah is two years older.
   c. Jasmine is two years older.
   d. Jasmine and Noah are twins.

3. Why did Noah and Jasmine move to the seashore?
   a. Their grandfather lived there.
   b. They went to learn to swim.
   c. They went to write a mystery story.
   d. Their parents got jobs there.

4. What kind of house did the family move to?
   a. an old, rundown shack
   b. a new little cottage
   c. a brick house right on the beach
   d. a large house with a spacious lawn

5. Why did the Dorns get the house for a low rent?

    a. It was Mr. López's house.

    b. People said bad things about the house.

    c. Mom and Dad had good jobs in the house.

    d. The Pinkneys were moving far away.

6. What happened first?

    a. The family moved to the house on Wendell Street.

    b. Jasmine and Noah got teased after school.

    c. Jasmine and Noah searched in old newspapers.

    d. Mrs. Dorn found a new job in Oceanside.

7. Why did the smugglers want to get even with the Pinkney family?

    a. The Pinkneys told the police about the smuggling.

    b. Mr. Pinkney made more money than other people.

    c. The Pinkneys tried to sink the smugglers' boats.

    d. Mr. López liked the Pinkneys better.

8. What happened in 1890?

    a. The Pinkneys disappeared.

    b. Mr. López started a newspaper.

    c. The house on Wendell Street was built.

    d. Zeke Little disappeared.

9. What is a good name for this selection?

    a. Seagulls

    b. The Unlucky House

    c. Jasmine's Cut Foot

    d. The New School

10. What is the selection mainly about?

    a. how they found out what happened to the Dorns

    b. how they found out what happened to the Pinkneys

    c. how they learned not to care about being teased

    d. how to look up information at the town hall

11. What was the best clue to solve the mystery?

    a. Mr. López's old newspapers

    b. a child's drawing

    c. the plans at the town hall

    d. some old letters

12. Why were the shells thought to be a treasure?

    a. They were in a painting.

    b. They were made of gold.

    c. They were rare.

    d. They were in boxes.

13. What was the best treasure Jasmine and Noah found?

    a. the bucket and the chain

    b. a trip back to the city

    c. some rare gold jewelry

    d. happiness in their new home

B **Find the correct word for each meaning. Write the words.**

searching	exclaimed	smugglers	despise
taxes	silent	teased	complain
discover	bucket	coins	rare
reward	grounds	basement	faded

1. not saying a word _____

2. money paid to a state or country _____

3. people who bring in goods from other lands without paying taxes

   _____

4. hate _____

5. looking for _____

6. made fun of _____

7. said in a surprised and excited way _____

8. prize given for good work _____

9. cents, such as pennies and dimes _____

10. very seldom found _____

11. to find out about something _____

12. underground floor of a house _____

13. lost color and got lighter _____

14. the land around a house _____

When we read a paragraph, most of the details tell something about a main idea. This main idea is in the topic sentence of the paragraph. The details tell more about the main idea.

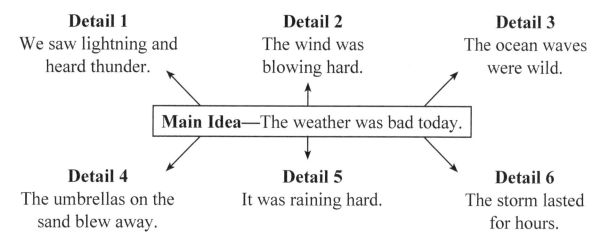

Detail 1
We saw lightning and heard thunder.

Detail 2
The wind was blowing hard.

Detail 3
The ocean waves were wild.

Main Idea—The weather was bad today.

Detail 4
The umbrellas on the sand blew away.

Detail 5
It was raining hard.

Detail 6
The storm lasted for hours.

Read each group of sentences below. Pick out the main idea in each group and label it *M.I.* Label each detail *D.*

1.

_____ **a.** Tiny plants and animals called plankton float near the top.

_____ **b.** Fish, squid, octopuses, and whales in the ocean eat plankton.

_____ **c.** The sea is home to millions of plants and animals.

_____ **d.** Animals as different as jellyfish, stingrays, eels, and sharks can be found in oceans.

_____ **e.** Different kinds of seaweed grow in the ocean and become food for sea animals.

2.

_____ **a.** The Pacific Ocean is the largest and deepest ocean and covers half the world.

_____ **b.** The smallest ocean is the cold, icy Arctic Ocean in the far north.

_____ **c.** The Atlantic Ocean, which reaches from America to Europe and Africa, is the second largest ocean.

_____ **d.** The third largest ocean, the Indian Ocean, goes from the eastern side of Africa and southern Asia to the cold frozen Antarctic.

_____ **e.** Salty ocean water covers most of the world.

D **Read each paragraph. Then read the three topic sentences. Underline the correct topic sentence for each paragraph.**

1.   Alligators and crocodiles are members of the reptile class of animals. Turtles are also reptiles. Snakes are members of the same class. Lizards are included, too.

    a. Crocodiles, lizards, and turtles are in the alligator class of animals.

    b. Only snakes and lizards are in the reptile class of animals.

    c. The reptile class has several different animals in it.

2.   Reptiles are cold-blooded. This means that their body temperature is the same as the place they are in. In hot deserts, reptiles' body temperature is high. In snow, their temperatures become very low. They go under the ground to keep from freezing.

    a. Reptiles seldom become hot.

    b. This is the way all reptiles are alike.

    c. Cold-blooded animals always have low temperatures.

3.   Snakes have no legs, but lizards have four short legs. Lizards have eyelids, though snakes have none. If you look at a lizard's head, you can see ears. Snakes do not have ears. Most snakes have one lung, but lizards have two lungs.

    a. Lizards and snakes are different from crocodiles.

    b. Snakes do not have eyelids, but most other animals do.

    c. It is not hard to tell the difference between snakes and lizards.

4.   The bottom scales of snakes are very smooth, so they can slide easily. Snakes also can swim and climb. They can jump through the air from tree to tree. They can move without using legs.

    a. Snakes are able to move in several ways.

    b. Snakes have no legs, eyelids, or ears.

    c. Snakes can climb trees and leap from tree to tree.

E When people read newspapers, first they look at the headlines. The headline tells the main idea of each article. If the headline is interesting, a person will usually read the article.

Choose the correct headline for each article below. Write the headline above the article. Then follow the directions.

HEADLINES

Wreckers Uncover 100-Year-Old Fortune

100 Pretzels Bring Medal, Money, and Salty Lips

70-Mile-an-Hour Winds Destroy 100 Homes

100 Furs Disappear Through Hole in Roof

_____

_____

1.   Workers wrecking an old building at 2758 Thorn Avenue uncovered a secret safe early today. The safe was hidden in an old chimney. When opened, the safe was found to hold a small jar filled with gold coins dating from 1840 to 1848. The jar was wrapped in a newspaper with the date of August 20, 1914. It is thought that the person who hid this treasure forgot about it.

_____

_____

2.   A sudden windstorm caused thousands of dollars of damage in Fairfield late yesterday afternoon. Seventy-mile-an-hour winds, with hail and strong rains, ripped the roofs off more than 200 homes. About half of these buildings were destroyed.

_____

_____

3.   Keisha West, age 10, of 98 Daffodil Court was the winner of the annual pretzel-eating contest. Miss West gobbled down 100 of the salty goodies in 40 minutes. The runner-up was Jacob Gray, who ate 99 pretzels. Keisha's prizes included a medal and a check for $25.

4. Write your own headline and a short paragraph to go with it below.

_____

_____

_____

_____

_____

_____

_____

F **The selection has several expressions in which the words do not mean exactly what they say. The expressions are often used, and people usually know the meaning. Here are examples:**

a. It is time to <u>take a break</u>. This means it is time to rest.

b. It took a long time, but then Jasmine <u>saw the light</u>. This means that at last Jasmine understood.

The following are expressions from the selection. Write the letter of the correct meaning next to each expression.

_____ **1.** The smugglers had promised to <u>get even with</u> the Pinkneys.

_____ **2.** "Look what a nice place we're getting for <u>next to nothing</u>," said Dad.

_____ **3.** The children complained to their parents and insisted they move, but <u>got nowhere.</u>

_____ **4.** The children did not <u>voice</u> their fears to each other.

_____ **5.** There was no way his parents could <u>turn down</u> cheap rent.

_____ **6.** She did not know when to <u>give up</u>.

Meanings

a. very little

b. stop fighting it

c. get back at

d. speak about

e say "no" to

f. did by oneself

g. did not succeed

Name _____ Date _____

---

1. A **fact** is a *true* piece of information. You must be able to prove your facts by showing where you found the information.

2. An **opinion** is what someone *thinks* about a topic. An opinion is not always a fact. This is because people have different opinions about the same topic.

G **This is one of the houses the Dorns looked at before they moved to Oceanside. Read what some neighbors said about this old house. Label each statement** *fact* **or** *opinion***.**

_____ 1. "It feels to me like that house is haunted."

_____ 2. "That house has broken windows."

_____ 3. "That house may give you nightmares."

_____ 4. "The house needs a paint job."

_____ 5. "It is dangerous for kids to play on the broken floors."

_____ 6. "I saw a rat run out of that house."

_____ 7. "I think that an old house like that is interesting."

_____ 8. "The owner of this house moved away from Oceanside."

Skills Review: Selections 7–12

The Tiger Swallowtail Butterfly

A tiger swallowtail butterfly has a little different life than other butterflies. The larva comes out of an egg laid on a green leaf. At that time it does not look like the usual caterpillar. It looks like a piece of black, brown, and white dirt. This is lucky for the larva. Birds do not look at it.

The larva chews on leaves and gets fat. Twice the larva sheds its old skin. Each time the new skin is greener. The third skin makes it look like a green caterpillar. But, again, it is able to fool birds. The green caterpillar has two spots on its head. These black, yellow, and white spots look like a snake's eyes. Birds that do not eat snakes will not bother the larva. The larva continues to eat and grow.

Soon the larva, or caterpillar, spins a silky thread. With the thread it fastens itself to a tree. Then the larva spins and covers its entire body with a cocoon. The pupa, or cocoon, looks like a piece of tree bark. It hangs on a twig and blends in with the tree.

When the adult butterfly bursts out of the cocoon, it is changed in color. It is no longer green but is now a black and yellow tiger swallowtail. Some females are black and blue in color. They look like a kind of butterfly that birds do not eat. Again, the birds are fooled.

A **Underline the correct answer to each question.**

1. When does the pupa stage come?

   a. after the larva stage

   b. before the larva stage

   c. before the egg stage

2. When does the butterfly look like a piece of dirt?

   a. during the pupa stage

   b. when it is in the egg

   c. during the larva stage

3. How does looking like a piece of dirt help the insect?

   a. Birds ignore it instead of eating it.

   b. It can easily travel in the breeze.

   c. It fools other kinds of butterflies.

4. When does the caterpillar attach itself to a tree?

    a. after it spins a cocoon

    b. when it is an adult

    c. before it spins a cocoon

5. When is the tiger swallowtail butterfly a green caterpillar?

    a. as soon as it hatches out of the egg

    b. before it looks like a piece of dirt

    c. after it looks like a piece of dirt

6. When do tiger swallowtails fool birds?

    a. only in the adult stage

    b. in the larva, pupa, and adult stages

    c. only when it looks like a piece of dirt

7. When do butterflies have snake-eye spots?

    a. when they are larvae

    b. when they are pupae

    c. when they are eggs

8. How do snake-eye spots keep the butterfly alive?

    a. They help the butterfly see its surroundings.

    b. They help the butterfly scare away its enemies.

    c. They help the butterfly hunt for food.

111

Name _____   Date _____

B **Below is a page from a dictionary. Use it to answer the following questions.**

> **cab • i • net** (kab′ i net) **1** *n*: a set of drawers **2** *n*: a piece of furniture with doors
>
> **cham • pi • on** (cham′ pē un) **1** *n*: one who defends weaker people **2** *n*: any person or thing that is best **3** *v*: to defend a person or idea
>
> **clue** (kloo̅) **1** *n*: something to help solve a problem **2** *n*: a hint
>
> **coast** (kōst) **1** *n*: land at the edge of the sea **2** *v*: to slide downhill on snow or ice
>
> **cob • bler** (kob′ lər) **1** *n*: a mender of shoes **2** *n*: a fruit pie made with a thick crust
>
> **cure** (kyur) **1** *n*: a way of healing a sick person **2** *v*: to make someone healthy again

1. How many meanings are given for the word *cabinet*? _____

2. How many syllables are in the word *champion*? _____

3. Which words have only one syllable each? _____

4. Which entry is a kind of dessert? _____

5. What are the correct guide words for this page? _____

6. List the entry words found on this dictionary page.

   _____

   _____

7. Which meaning of the word *cobbler* is used in this sentence?

   The cobbler bought leather to fix the boot.

   _____

8. Which meaning of the word *coast* is used in this sentence?

   We watched the people <u>coast</u> on the bobsled.

   _____

9. Which meaning of the word *coast* is a noun?

   _____

Skills Review: Selections 7–12
Core Skills Reading Comprehension, Grade 4

10. Is *cure* used as a noun or a verb in this sentence?

Veterinarians work to <u>cure</u> animal diseases.

C **Synonyms are words with similar meanings. Write each word from the box next to its synonym.**

antique	ask	complain
despised	exclaimed	fight
hunt	hurt	laughed
pebbles	port	thing
unsafe	unusual	wail

1. hated _____

2. old _____

3. harbor _____

4. search _____

5. struggle _____

6. shouted _____

7. injure _____

8. grumble _____

9. inquire _____

10. strange _____

11. object _____

12. stones _____

13. moan _____

14. dangerous _____

15. giggled _____

D Zari and Deon are from Greenville. They are in the fourth grade. Here are some things that their classmates said about them. Some are facts. Some are opinions. Read each statement and label it either *opinion* or *fact*. The first one is done for you.

Zari helped me write a book report.

1. fact

Deon has a hole in his jeans.

2. _____

Deon is the best-looking boy in Greenville.

3. _____

Zari won her tennis match.

4. _____

Zari failed the last math test.

5. _____

Deon mows the lawn on Saturdays.

6. _____

I think Deon is the best artist in fourth grade.

7. _____

I love the color of Zari's sneakers.

8. _____

Deon tried out for the basketball team.

9. _____

Name _____ Date _____

 Read the following article about the *onager*. Then write the correct details in the outline below. Be sure to write a title for the outline.

Onager is the name of an animal in the horse family. It is wild and travels in a herd. The onager looks very much like a donkey. In the summer it is dark brown, but in the winter its fur coat turns to yellowish-brown. It has a black stripe down its back. The onager has a mane. At the end of its tail is a tuft of hair.

Herds of onagers can be found on the hot, dry grasslands of central Asia. They are very fast runners. Traveling in herds and running fast help protect onagers from their enemies. The way their fur changes in the seasons also protects onagers.

Title: _____

    I. What the onanger looks like

        A. _____

        B. _____

        C. _____

        D. _____

    II. How the onager protects itself

        A. _____

        B. _____

        C. _____

   III. Where onagers are found

        A. _____

        B. _____

Answer Key

Selection 1
Pages 1–7

A 1. c
   2. b
   3. a
   4. a
   5. b
   6. d

B 1. afraid, nervous
   2. bounded, hopped
   3. sleepy, weary
   4. splashing, wading
   5. considered, reflected
   6. calming, relaxing
   7. grouchy, grumpy
   8. bumpy, rough

C 1. Sample answer: The rabbit warns the crocodile not to talk about trouble that way.
   2. Sample answer: The flamingo flies up in the air and startles the monkey.
   3. Sample answer: The monkey knocks over the cake and starts a grass fire.
   4. Sample answer: The crocodile gets burned by the grass fire.
   5. Sample answer: The crocodile got burned by the trouble he caused.

D 1. …the crocodile's back was as soft and smooth as a little child's cheek.
   2. …the crocodile's back has been bumpy…
   3. "I never have trouble. In fact, I bet Trouble would be afraid to bother me."
   4. The more he thought, the more angry he became. At last, he decided to go find Trouble and tell him to mind his own business.

E Possible answers: The crocodile says that Trouble would be afraid to bother him. The crocodile goes looking for Trouble to tell him to mind his own business. The crocodile's anger frightens the flamingo, which causes trouble to occur.

Selection 2
Pages 8–16

A 1. c
   2. b
   3. d
   4. b
   5. d

B 1. Chipmunk thinks Bear is foolish for believing he can control the sun.
   2. Bear sees the sun rising.
   3. Bear pins Chipmunk to the ground.
   4. Chipmunk squirms free of Bear's paw.
   5. The tips of Bear's claws scrape Chipmunk's back.

C 1. healed
   2. squirm
   3. snuggled
   4. glow
   5. reminder
   6. rise
   7. glow
   8. squirm
   9. healed
   10. reminder
   11. snuggled
   12. rise

D Answers will vary but should be accurate descriptions of each character.

E Answers will vary but should be good examples for each category.

F 1. c
   2. b
   3. a
   4. d
   5. b
   6. c

G 1. Crocodile goes looking for Trouble.
   2. Crocodile frightens the flamingo. Flamingo startles the monkey. Monkey knocks over cake and causes fire. Fire burns the crocodile.
   3. Crocodile has a bumpy back.
   4. Bear pins Chipmunk to the ground.
   5. Chipmunk tells Bear that he was just kidding. Chipmunk tells Bear that the sun changed its mind and is going down.
   6. Chipmunk has stripes on his back.

Selection 3
Pages 17–21

A 1. d
   2. b
   3. a
   4. c
   5. b
   6. c

Answer Key
Core Skills Reading Comprehension, Grade 4

B 1. harbor
   2. clumsy
   3. trophies
   4. surface
   5. champion
   6. wilted
   7. compete/struggle
   8. advise
   9. toured
   10. toddled

Selection 4
Pages 22–26

A 1. b
   2. d
   3. d
   4. a
   5. b, c, e
   6. b
   7. b

B First column: Wayne swims laps in the pool every morning

Second column: Mr. and Mrs. Bell stopped watching Denise for a minute

Third column: Wayne dove in the water to save Denise from drowning. Wayne and Rudy's class takes a tour of sailing ships. Wayne and Rudy use their strong swimming skills.

C 1. Rita is the best swimmer on the team.
   2. The Greeks and Romans taught their children to swim early in life.
   3. It was not until 1850 that people found that they could put themselves in water without becoming ill.
   4. "This is certainly not my lucky day!" exclaimed Rudy.
   5. These are the main differences between houseboats and other types of boats.

D Answers will vary but should include details to support each topic sentence.

E 1. The woman teaches in my school. A dolphin is not really a fish.
   2. People like to go to the library. Some people have trouble singing.

Selection 5
Pages 27–36

A 1. d
   2. c
   3. c

   4. a
   5. b
   6. b
   7. b
   8. d
   9. d
   10. a
   11. b

B 1. detective
   2. apartment
   3. captain
   4. brag
   5. collected
   6. flashlight
   7. autumn
   8. diamond
   9. stole
   10. thermos
   11. army
   12. jewels

C 1. c
   2. b
   3. a

D 1. third person
   2. third person
   3. first person
   4. third person
   5. first person

Underline the following:
   1. she, his
   2. he, his
   3. we, I, my
   4. their, they
   5. my, I

E 1. b
   2. b
   3. a
   4. c
   5. c
   6. a
   7. d
   8. c
   9. e
   10. Answers will vary.
   11. c
   12. d
   13. b
   14. a

117

Selection 6
Pages 37–48

A 1. a
   2. c
   3. b
   4. c
   5. c
   6. d
   7. b
   8. b
   9. d
   10. c
   11. c
   12. d
   13. d
   14. c
   15. Answers will vary.

B 1. veterinarian
   2. valuable
   3. antiques
   4. explain
   5. amazement
   6. grumble or moan
   7. objects
   8. explore
   9. moan
   10. sale
   11. skinny
   12. weak
   13. gentle

C 1. c, e
   2. b
   3. a. The show is free.
      b. The antique fair will be held at Harbor Hall in Marble City.
      c. The fair will be held on Friday, November 3, from 8–10 P.M.
      d. They can buy antiques.
   4. a and d
   5. a. Anna Hoodidit and Phil O'Chuckles
      b. Two Hundred Old Jokes
      c. The Mystery of the Antique Box
      d. The Life of a Quarterback and Fishing Made Easy
      e. Susan Young Collector

D 1. London
   2. about 175 years ago
   3. His parents died and there was no one to take care of him.
   4. from scraps and coins people gave him
   5. old coins

6. He helped Tom sell the coins
7. the woman at the bakery
8. They were antique Roman coins, not English money.
9. He sold the coins.
10. to give Hudson the cat back to his owner

E Sentences will vary but should include accurate details about Tom Tyler and Hudson.

F 1. c
   2. f
   3. a
   4. g
   5. i
   6. h
   7. d

Skills Review: Selections 1–6
Pages 49–54

A 1. State House
   2. Market Street
   3. west
   4. south
   5. Tannery
   6. State House Inn
   7. Possible response: Go west on Market Street and turn left (or south) on Fourth Street. Cross Chestnut Street and look for Tannery on your left.
   8. Seventh Street

B 1. Polly, Molly, Dolly
   2. a. Sign 2
   b. Sign 1
   c. for repairs
   d. April 4–April 18; two weeks or 14 days
   e. on March 18
   f. count the marbles in the jar and fill out an entry form
   g. carnival tickets
   h. by falling bricks

C 1. sick
   2. by himself
   3. say "no"
   4. start a conversation
   5. understood
   6. look into

D 1. M.I. – a; D – b, c, d, e
   2. M.I. – d; D – a, b, c, e
   3. M.I. – c; D – a, b, d, e

E Monkeys' paws are useful tools.

118

F 1. Nome is a city in the state of Alaska. Moles also live deep in the earth and dig for food.
    2. Columbus traveled many miles on his trips. After their return to the north, robins begin to build nests.

G 1. c
    2. b
    3. a
    4. b

Selection 7
Pages 55–61

A 106

B 1. c
    2. d
    3. c
    4. a
    5. c
    6. b
    7. a
    8. b

C 1. two
    2. three
    3. large, yellowish-pink fish with silvery scales
    4. plates covering fish and some animals
    5. sable
    6. sale–selling at lower prices than usual
    7. a piece of cloth attached to a ship's mast so the wind will move the ship
    8. sail, sale
    9. scale
    10. sandpaper

D Check ✓ sentences 1, 4, 5, 7, 10, 11, 12, 13.
Mark **X** by sentences 2, 3, 6, 8, 9, 14, 15.

E Sentences will vary.

F 1. manager
    2. strange
    3. inquire
    4. problem
    5. giggle

Selection 8
Pages 62–70

A 1. b
    2. d
    3. b
    4. d
    5. c
    6. d
    7. a
    8. c

B Across
    1. fangs
    4. trample
    5. forked
    9. temperature

    Down
    2. swallow
    3. cannibal
    6. prey
    7. lungs
    8. venom

C Outlines may vary.
    I. Body parts of snakes
      A. No eyelids or feet
      B. Forked tongues
      C. Scales
      D. Lungs
      E. Fangs
    III. How a snake eats
      A. Swallows prey whole
      B. Jaws that spread wide
      C. Bulges in body
    IV. What a snake eats
      A. Eggs
      B. Rats
      C. Toads
      D. Insects
      E. Other snakes
    V. Enemies of snakes
      A. Human beings
      B. Large birds
      C. Pigs
      D. Other snakes
    VI. Where snakes are found
      A. Ponds
      B. Streams
      C. Gardens
      D. Woods
      E. Swamps
      F. Jungles

D Outlines may vary.
    Fleas
    I. Why fleas are dangerous
      A. Spread diseases to humans
      B. Spread diseases to animals
      C. Make people and animals uncomfortable
    II. What fleas look like
      A. Flat, short, pale
      B. No wings
      C. Strong hind legs for jumping
      D. Long, sharp, sucking beak

119

III. Where fleas live
   A. On animals' fur
   B. Places animals sleep
   C. In birds' feathers
   D. Rugs and carpets
   E. Cracks in floors
IV. How fleas eat
   A. Make hole in skin of prey
   B. Suck blood of prey

Selection 9
Pages 71–79

A 1. d
   2. a
   3. b
   4. c
   5. c
   6. c
   7. a
   8. b
   9. c
   10. b
   11. a
   12. d

B 1. quill
   2. cocoon
   3. peanuts
   4. caterpillar
   5. parchment
   6. pearls
   7. ballpoint pen
   8. oyster
   9. felt-tipped pens

C 1. butterfly
   2. pupa
   3. life
   4. cocoon
   5. peg
   6. cocoon
   7. parchment
   8. peanut
   9. on stems under the ground
   10. skin
   11. feather
   12. sea animal
   13. speck of sand

D 1. c, b, a, d
   2. c, d, a, e, f, b

E 1. b, c
   2. b, d
   3. b, c
   4. a, b
   5. c, d
   6. a, b

F 2. The larva hatches from an egg.
   3. The greedy caterpillar eats and eats.
   4. The caterpillar sheds its skin.
   5. The caterpillar spins a cocoon.
   6. The pupa hangs quietly in the cocoon.
   7. The butterfly bursts out of its cocoon.
   8. The butterfly dries out.
   9. The adult butterfly flies away.

Selection 10
Pages 80–86

A 1. b
   2. c
   3. d
   4. a
   5. c
   6. b
   7. c
   8. b

B 1. 12
   2. Pu–Rh
   3. A–Bo
   4. 1
   5. 11
   6. So–Tu
   7. 5
   8. Va–Zy
   9. a. 10, Sc–Sn
      b. 3, Ea–Ga
      c. 2, Br–Du
      d. 3, Ea–Ga
      e. 3, Ea–Ga
      f. 1, A–Bo
      g. 12, Va–Zy
      h. 1, A–Bo

C 1. b
   2. a
   3. d
   4. c

D 1. b, e
   2. c
   3. d

120

Selection 11
Pages 87–95

A
1. b
2. d
3. d
4. c
5. c
6. c
7. a
8. b
9. c
10. b
11. d
12. c
13. c

B
1. admire
2. upright
3. modern
4. emerald
5. judge
6. banker
7. stable
8. mayor
9. monster
10. gramophone
11. outdo
12. dirty
13. informed

C
1. b, e
2. b
3. b, f
4. d
5. b
6. b
7. b
8. a
9. b, e
10. b
11. d
12. c

D
1. one minute
2. one day
3. one year
4. one hour
5. one year
6. one month
7. one month
8. one week
9. six months
10. forty-two days
11. thirty
12. thirty

Selection 12
Pages 96–109

A
1. d
2. b
3. d
4. d
5. b
6. d
7. a
8. d
9. b
10. b
11. b
12. c
13. d

B
1. silent
2. taxes
3. smugglers
4. despise
5. searching
6. teased
7. exclaimed
8. reward
9. coins
10. rare
11. discover
12. basement
13. faded
14. grounds

C
1. a. D
   b. D
   c. M.I.
   d. D
   e. D
2. a. D
   b. D
   c. D
   d. D
   e. M.I.

D
1. c
2. b
3. c
4. a

E
1. Wreckers Uncover 100-Year-Old Fortune
2. 70-Mile-an-Hour Winds Destroy 100 Homes
3. 100 Pretzels Bring Medal, Money, and Salty Lips
4. Responses will vary but should include a headline that tells the main idea or topic of the paragraph.

121

F 1. c
2. a
3. g
4. d
5. e
6. b

G 1. opinion
2. fact
3. opinion
4. fact
5. fact
6. fact
7. opinion
8. fact

Skills Review: Selections 7–12
Pages 110–115

A 1. a
2. c
3. a
4. c
5. c
6. b
7. a
8. b

B 1. two
2. three
3. clue, coast, cure
4. cobbler
5. cabinet, cure
6. cabinet, champion, clue, coast, cobbler, cure
7. 1. a mender of shoes
8. 2. to slide downhill on snow or ice
9. 1. land at the edge of the sea
10. verb

C 1. despised
2. antique
3. port
4. hunt
5. fight
6. exclaimed
7. hurt
8. complain
9. ask
10. unusual
11. thing
12. pebbles
13. wail
14. unsafe
15. laughed

D 2. fact
3. opinion
4. fact
5. fact
6. fact
7. opinion
8. opinion
9. fact

E Outlines may vary.

Facts About the Onanger
I. A. Like a donkey
B. Black stripe down back
C. Has a mane
D. Tuft of hair at end of tail
II. A. Travels in herds
B. Are very fast runners
C. Fur changes color so it cannot be easily seen
III. A. Hot, dry grasslands
B. Central Asia

122

Printed in the USA
CPSIA information can be obtained
at www.ICGtesting.com
CBHW081410050724
11187CB00041B/1107